ON THE ROAD WITH SEAN OF THE SOUTH

SEAN DIETRICH

Copyright © 2016 Sean Dietrich

All rights reserved.

ISBN-13:978-1975746278

ISBN-10:1975746279

DEDICATION

To my wife, Jamie, without her I'd never arrive anywhere on time. And to each one of my readers, who evidently have poor taste in literature, but very big hearts. Thank you.

THANK YOU

I thank my mama for everything she is. I thank her most especially for believing in me even when I didn't.

A REDHEAD DOES PACE HIGH SCHOOL

We drove toward the Smoky Mountains of North Carolina for Thanksgiving. We have been spending holidays with family ever since the earth cooled. We had never been alone. But on this particular holiday we would take as a two-person-one-dog family to the mountains.

We rode the highways toward North Carolina with a foul-smelling coonhound sleeping in the front seat between us. We pulled over for the utmost important side-of-the-road attractions. Such as, the Case Pocketknife Outlet, various boiled peanut stands, and the world's largest Duncan Phyfe chair.

I love this particular drive. Always have. As a boy, we used to visit my aunt and uncle in North Carolina. I have nothing but happy memories here. I remembered visiting Mount Airy—also known as Mayberry—and getting my picture taken outside Floyd's Barbershop. I sat at the holy desk, pretending to be Andy for a few minutes.

My aunt's house was a small one. It smelled funny, and had couches that were covered in plastic. One particular day, I went figure-skating on her slick, linoleum kitchen floor. I attempted a double Axel. The crowd went wild. Then, the triple Axel. The millions of fans screamed. All tens from the judges. Then, the double Lutz. "Can he do it?" said Eli Gold in his radio voice. "I don't know, Tom," said Eli. "It's been a long night."

My acrobatics wounded me. I slid shin-first into my aunt's gas heater. A jagged piece of rusted metal cut my calf muscle clean across.

Three maternal women loaded a fallen redheaded boy into my aunt's Plymouth and drove me to the hospital.

My mother had wrapped my leg in a trash bag so I wouldn't get blood in my aunt's backseat. My aunt flaunted the law and sped through the three caution lights to the hospital.

The physician who stitched me up was tall, he looked like Charlton Heston, with spectacles. He told me he would reward me with something very special if I didn't cry while he worked on me.

It's not every day a member of the establishment offers to reward you. So, I grit my teeth when he shoved a three-foot-long needle into my leg. I bit my lip when he sewed me up with thread. I reminded myself about a coming reward.

When it was finished, I waited with my hands in my lap like a good little redhead. I reminded the nurse that I wore a size medium, my favorite color was yellow, and I preferred my poundcake slices to be fat.

The doctor came into the room. He smiled at me. He quoted the Sermon on the Mount by memory. From the first word to the last. Then, he patted my shoulder and said, "That was your reward, son. The words of the Good Shepherd."

I haven't trusted a single doctor since.

So our trip. We were having a nice drive. But when my wife crossed the Georgia-North Carolina border, something was wrong. The air in the distance was thick and gray. There were no majestic mountains to be seen —they were covered in smoke. The farther we drove into the Tar Heel State, the more I felt like I was riding in the passenger seat of an unfiltered Camel.

We pulled over at a gas station. The smoke made my eyes water. I walked inside to pay. The woman behind the counter wore a wet handkerchief around her face like an Old West train-bandit.

"Howdy," she said.

"What's all this smoke from?" I asked.

"Some kid's been starting forest fires up close to here. Fires got outta control, they haven't caught him yet, half the state's up in flames."

It was Armageddon for Thanksgiving.

When we arrived at our small cabin, we could hardly see through the blanket of smoke. I coughed while I unloaded luggage. I gasped, wheezed, hacked, and sniffed. The mountain-views were suppose to be incredible. And for all I know they might have been. But that week, they were invisible behind billows of heavenly judgement. Our clothes smelled like hickory. Our hair smelled like my aunt Delpha's ashtray. I wanted to go home.

The only folk-remedy that seemed to relieve my moderately-severe symptoms of general respiratory discomfort was beer.

Thus, on a miserable Thanksgiving night, while I self-administered a Budweiser, my wife cooked homemade chicken and dumplings while wearing a wet hanky around her face. Dumplings, you'll note, are one of my favorite things in the world. And my wife knows her way around a dumpling.

But because our heads were crammed with ten pounds of snot and soot, I could not taste a bite.

She went to bed early. I wished her a goodnight and a

Happy Thanksgiving. I passed the holiday evening, sitting perched by the cozy warmth and glow of the cabin's flatscreen television.

I watched reruns of the Andy Griffith Show late into night, and remembered my trips to Mount Airy as a boy. Whenever I see Floyd's Barbershop bench, I remember sitting there once and smiling for my mother's wind-up camera.

Before I went to bed that night, my cellphone made a noise. I paused Andy. It was an email, from a reader on my blog. Her name was Mrs. Bell. She taught at Pace High School. She wanted to know if I would speak to her students.

This gave me a laugh.

Speaking. Me. There are fewer things I would be worse suited for, I thought. Such as: emptying porta-Johns, moving birdbaths, or playing semi-professional Cricket.

I was no public speaker. Furthermore, I had nothing of any value to say to high-school kids—and no business pretending like I did.

And that's exactly what I meant to type in a response to Mrs. Bell. I really did. But the smoke was getting to me.

So I accepted her offer.

~

It was early morning. Pace High School sat situated across from a peanut field. My wife and I walked inside the old building and wandered through the hallways which were adorned with a thousand photos of school alumni.

Mrs. Bell had organized everything. A tour, introductions, and even a breakfast for me and my wife. The breakfast would be a meet-and-greet with Pace High faculty. I expected three or four people standing around a box of donuts, sipping coffee, discussing how to scrub oil-spots off residential driveways. I was sorely mistaken.

There were roughly—and this is just a guesstimate—six hundred thousand people there. They were all strangers, but they all seemed to know me. They formed a single-file line and took turns pumping my hand, hugging my neck, kissing my cheeks, and handing me books to sign.

Me. Signing books. I had never signed anything more than a tax-return. And to be quite honest, it felt utterly ridiculous.

"Make this book out to Phyllis," said one teacher. "That's my grandmother, she's ninety, she reads you."

You could've knocked me over with a lint-roller.

During the span of a few minutes, I got so many hugs, my shoulder hurt. I never did get to eat breakfast.

I understand there were homemade biscuits on the buffet line—it remains one of the great disappointments of my life.

Later that day, I spoke to groups of students in the library. They were high-schoolers of all kinds. Some were awkward-looking and excited. Others were quiet and shy. Some were smart and had bright futures ahead of them. Others were poor, unfortunate souls who wanted to be writers.

So, I spoke. I talked about myself and told stories. I did a pathetic job. I wasn't used to telling these stories to anyone but my wife or a qualified psychiatrist. And it was there, standing before Pace High's finest, that I realized my writings weren't just letters on a computer screen. They were my story.

And something happened to me, standing in front of innocent children who held *my* books in their hands.

I felt humbled.

Afterward, I got comments from kids. One boy told me his father had just died. A young girl hugged me and told me she missed her sister who'd passed in a car accident. An older gentleman who looked like a retired linebacker shook my hand and thanked me for being me. One girl told me she felt like an outsider, and wanted to be a writer—she and I kept in touch via email. Another boy hugged me and asked if I would ever be back.

I guess what I'm trying to say is: they treated me like I was some*body*. And I've never had the delusional persuasions to consider myself as anything more than a *no*body.

When it was over, Mrs. Bell walked us to our vehicle in the parking lot. She handed me a cardboard box. In the box were baseball caps, T-shirts, jackets, and camouflage hunting gear—all bearing the Pace High logo.

Then, she presented me with a baseball, signed by Addison Russel. Russel was the most valuable player during that years' World Series. And this got me excited. I am a baseball fanatic.

"Addison Russel graduated from Pace," she told me. "We all thought this would be something you'd really like."

It was.

My wife and I ate a late lunch at a country restaurant afterward. The place was nearly empty, except for Patsy Cline on the stereo system. Our waitress looked too old to be in the business.

Before our food arrived, neither my wife nor I said much to each other. I was still in shock from the festivities, I guess. Until that day, I'd never really met any of my readers face-to-face.

I held the autographed baseball and turned it in my hands.

"How're you feeling?" asked my wife.

"Tired," said I. "A little drained."

It was one of the best feelings I'd ever had in my cotton-picking life. Even better than the time I couple-skated with Krystal Fortner at the ripe age of ten. I was still a terrible public speaker, of course. I knew I'd never be invited to speak anywhere else, and would probably never have another day like the euphoric one I had in the sleepy town of Pace.

My wife was busy on her smartphone while I stared out the window at the traffic rolling through Santa Rosa County.

"We just got another email," my wife said. "They want you to come speak in Birmingham."

COUNTRY COME TO TOWN

A Pennsylvania concert hall. There I am, on a stage. I have a guitar in my hands. I am playing music and telling stories to a crowd of people who look like normal human beings. But they aren't. They're Pennsylvanians.

I've never been to Pennsylvania before. And I can't say I will ever be back. I have nothing against the state. And I have nothing against the people. But this place feels like Mars.

People speak with nasal accents that sound like Hitler giving a wedding toast. I don't recognize *any* of the trees. A man flipped me off in traffic because I didn't accelerate fast enough at a green light.

The Pennsylvanian towns are frightening. Earlier today, I walked into a music store to buy guitar picks for tonight's show. The man behind the counter had a cigar in his mouth and was reading a newspaper.

I asked if he had any guitar picks.

He lowered the newsprint and said, "*GEE*-tar picks?" he said, doing a poor imitation of me. "You aren't from around here, are you?"

"*Ain't* from around here," I corrected him.

We hit it off.

He gave me the tour of his music store and told me about himself. His name was Brick, and even though he was a cranky Yankee who didn't love the Lord, he sure could pick a mean *gee*-tar.

That day, my friend took me to a Polish restaurant for lunch. It was a strange place. Until then, the only Polish food I'd ever had was a sausage served at my cousin's fortieth-birthday cookout. This fare was different. And, to add insult to injury, there were no baked beans. Only odd concoctions of cabbage, which had been stewed for a minimum of seventy-two years. And unusual-looking eye-ball-shaped deals called *pierogies*.

"What're these?" I said, stabbing my fork at the *pierogy* on my plate.

"Those're kinda like dumplings," said my friend.

Dumplings my ass.

My poor, misguided Pennsylvanian friend. This lump of white was no dumpling. A dumpling is something mama rolls on a counter with a rolling pin, then adds to a pot of boiling chicken. When people eat *her* dumplings, hatred is eradicated from the face of the planet, world peace is actuated, and somewhere in the world, Jimmy Carter smiles.

This lump was no dumpling. It tasted like a pig's prostate wrapped in a ravioli shell.

I went to the concert hall for a soundcheck. It was raining. The musicians and storytellers who went on before me were animals of a different color. They made fun of my beat-up guitar and my facial hair. The guitar I inherited from my daddy is special to me. My facial hair came from the same place the guitar did.

I shared a dressing room with a man who will remain nameless. But, I will tell you that he wears so much leather he squeaks when he walks. He demanded herbal tea before going onstage. The stage-hands brought him an entire rack of herb medleys. He was from somewhere up north, and he referred to anyone within a six-feet radius as *buddy*.

I dislike the nickname *buddy*.

The stage-hand asked if I wanted anything special. Teas, a sliced kiwi tray, or champagne served in copper goblets topped with Thousand Island dressing.

"Do you have any chicken and dumplings?" I asked.

"What're those?" she said.

"I think they're like *pierogies,*" offered the man in leather.

Leatherman went on stage before me. I saw his whole act. He told stories about his world travels. He talked about being on Oprah once—he had a lot to say about her. The crowd loved him. His high-pitched voice was a cross between a mafia hitman and two house cats mating in the backyard.

Then it's my turn.

I step onto a quiet stage to a hall full of crickets. And here I am.

Just look at me. I'm a skinny white boy with legs that are unnaturally long for his body, and hair that won't do what I tell it to do.

I'm telling stories about fishing in the Choctawhatchee Bay without my shoes on. I talk about developing the *ground-itch* one summer, when I stepped on dog dookie. And, when I explain that the *ground-itch* is, in fact, a bad case of hook-worm—which often brings in a few laughs—I am met with blank stares. As soon as I say "ringworm," a few people get up and leave.

So, I play my guitar. I sing songs from the Hank Williams Senior catalog to a bunch of Pennsylvanians who scratch their hindparts during the chorus.

Now, I'm talking about all the rural things I love. About rundown truck-stops, summer VBS programs in fifty-two-member churches. Moonrises in the woods. Homemade moonshine from a small-town lawyer who tries to earn extra money to pay for his kid's private school tuition. I talk about the kudzu that grows behind my aunt's house. About killing squirrels with a slingshot, and the proper way to prepare chicken and dumplings.

I finish my stories.

Lord help me. It's quiet in here. Quiet enough to hear a *pierogy* drop. I walk off the stage with my head down. A few people clap, but not everyone.

God bless that old woman on the front row who is clapping just as vigorously as my mother might.

After my act, I am followed by a comedian. A man who wears a three-piece suit, who discusses national politics while sipping whiskey. In his opening sentence, he uses the F-word. The place goes crazy. He tells a dirty joke. The room howls. He shows his middle finger to the sky and makes a remark about God and country. People ask for an encore.

After the show, an old woman finds me in the hallway backstage. She's the one who was clapping for me. She tells me she is from Houston County, Alabama. Her accent sounds like home.

She misses her childhood home so bad, she can't sleep sometimes.

"I been gone forty years," she says. "Only been back a few times, my kids all live up here in Pennsylvania, I wish they didn't."

She hugs me, and I can smell her perfume. It's the same kind of perfume my granny wore. I don't know what it's called, but I like it.

"Thank you for coming," she says. "Try not to hold anything against these people. They're good folks, just a little stiff."

Stiff? A few of them were flat-out embalmed.

On the plane ride home, I feel like a failure. I am feeling pretty low. It's hard to stand on stage and listen to audience members break wind after you tell a heartfelt story about your own life.

But then, the truth is, I am not a performer. I never

have been. In fact, I don't know how I've fallen into this line of work.

Maybe it's all some kind of mistake, I'm thinking. After all, it wasn't too long ago, I was buying six-packs in Walmart checkout aisles after swinging a hammer all day. It wasn't long ago, I was playing music at Danny's neighborhood bar, to a group of dangerously inebriated folks who were only there for the all-you-can-eat catfish. It wasn't long ago I was throwing newspapers with my mother at three in the morning.

When my plane touches down, the first thing I see are longleaf pines. I forget all bad feelings.

Sure. Maybe I have no business telling stories to Pennsylvanians. But right now I don't care about any of that. Because look at those trees.

Those pines have a way of cleaning troubled minds. They stretch from the crown of Florida to the southern tip of Virginia, and when I see them, I'm home.

When I smell them, I think of eighty-five-year-old Stuart Wood, who lived in a double-wide trailer a few dirt roads down from me. He played guitar like Chet Atkins.

I think of Jim Griffith—who has Alzheimer's now—who took me horseback riding and told me that I was a smart kid once.

I think of my baseball-playing friend Lyle Sandquist, who told me once, "Having fun is more fun than winning."

My wife meets me at the airport. She's standing with a smile on her face. We hug, and she smells like our house. She has coonhound hairs on her white blouse.

"I'm glad you're home," she says. "I made chicken and dumplings for supper."

AMERICA

I'm in an interstate truck stop drinking lukewarm coffee that tastes like bathwater. There are antlers on the wall near the Coke machine. My eggs are overdone, my bacon tastes like rubber, my vinyl seat has a tear in it.

This is heaven.

I'm watching television. On the screen: a gentleman in a suit complains about America.

"Sometimes, I hate America," the talking head says. "I don't even like our flag..."

The waitress slaps off the television.

A man at the counter shakes his head and cusses at the TV. I know what he's thinking because I'm thinking the same thing.

This talk-show host has the IQ of coleslaw.

Furthermore, I don't hate my homeland. I love everything from Spanish moss to Roy Rogers. From swamps to double-wide trailers to homemade moonshine.

Consequently, once in North Florida, someone gave me a jar of strawberry moonshine. The next morning, I awoke in South Alabama with a toothache.

I also like bass ponds, railroads, hog farms, vegetable stands, and flatbed Fords—I've owned six.

I like Bob Feller, Hank Aaron, and Ken Griffey Jr. I

like pigskin footballs, and coaches who make boys into men. I prefer cheap beer, and though I don't smoke, I love the smell of Virginian tobacco in Grandaddy's corncob pipe.

And if that's not patriotic enough, I love Hank, Merle, George, and Willie. I like Will Rogers, Bugs Bunny, Hee Haw, and Louis Armstrong. And whenever I hear a preacher deliver a Baptist-style message, I'm liable to stand and holler.

I'm not finished.

I love Savannah, Charleston, Milton, Jay, Pollard, Defuniak Springs, Valdosta, Grand Ridge, Palatka, Keithville, Greenwood, Lake City, Eastpoint, Wewahitchka, Brewton, Tuscaloosa, Dixonville, and Andalusia.

I like Martin guitars, Stetson hats, Buck knives, Winchester 1873's, and anyone who says, "y'all."

And when I hear the National Anthem, I don't give a damn which NFL football players throw tantrums about it. This is my home, I'm standing. Not just for my flag. For my grandaddy, who wore a purple heart, and still does—six feet beneath the soil.

I stand for those whose friends got butchered. For cotton-pickers, peanut farmers, and steel workers who believed in fifty-six signatures on a piece of parchment. For Mexican-Americans, blacks, whites, homosexuals, and anyone who can fog up a mirror. For those who love an idea so big and pure, they sing about it before ball games.

I'm not going to lie, I don't care for politics. I care even less for politicians who wouldn't know their own ass from a phonebook. But I love this truckstop, the antlers on the wall, the jukebox in the corner.

You.

And, by God, I love Old Glory.

SMALL TOWN FLORIDA

Last Saturday, I rode east on Florida Highway 100 until I ran smack-dab into a sign reading: "Welcome to Palatka."

Palatka is a faded town on the Saint Johns River, with so many mossy oaks it'll catch your breath. There's a downtown small enough to pitch a baseball through, and a diner named, Bradley's—which boasts the most mounted deer in the tri-county area.

It's political season in Palatka. Posters everywhere. One reads: "Elect Gator for sheriff." The sign beside it: "Crickets, red wigglers, ammunition, and boiled peanuts."

We stayed at a friend's house. Miss Leslie rolled out a spread. Her husband, Tank,—a goodhearted man who resembles a piece of military defense machinery—operated the deep-fryer.

And by dog, we had a party.

The buffet line had all the trimmings you'd expect in the deep South. Field peas with enough ham to make a cardiologist nervous. Venison, casseroles, deep-fried everything.

The conversation didn't follow any ground rules. One woman talked about the health benefits of cow pies. Miss Jane—distinguished English teacher and highly-decorated hell-raiser—recited a toast which made someone laugh so hard he swallowed his cigarette.

A group of fellas in the corner talked about the finer points of sausage. John told a story about when a hog bit off his buddy's finger.

Then, there's white-headed Nana, whose candy-apple red blouse and earrings matched her pocket book. She looks like the cover of a Better Homes and Gardens magazine—only sassier.

Nana said, "I feel lucky to have lived in Palatka all these years, it was a perfect place to raise children. And even though we don't have many shoe stores, we get by."

They do more than get by.

They live easy. Sure, they have problems, this isn't heaven. But it's pretty stinking close. If you don't believe me, you ought to visit the curbside stand that still sells raw honey using the honor system.

No thefts since 1947.

Well. Except for the incident when three high-schoolers stole the honey-stand's six-hundred-pound purple chicken with a pickup truck and towed it twenty-seven miles. One kid was spotted mounted on the bird, slapping its hindsection, riding down the road shouting, "Hi-ho Chicken, away!"

That kind of stuff doesn't happen in New Jersey.

This is a small town. A place where kids go barefoot, and people keep windows open. Where you don't need reasons to throw Saturday lawn parties. Where everyone knows everyone, where neighbors are cousins. Where out-of-towners get fed-to-death, and conversations end around two in the morning. Where love isn't cheap, but it's free if you want it.

You might think such things are a fantasy this day and age. They aren't.

They're just down the road.

MADE WITH LOVE

I'd give my left kidney for a piece of bacon right now. My wife is making breakfast as we speak, I can smell it in the other room—and hear it, too.

Long ago, I didn't think our morning meals were anything fancy—now I know they are. Though it's no thanks to me. She makes everything from scratch: biscuits, sausage gravy, hash browns, even jam. I do my part to help. I watch television for us both.

To be fair, I do buy our eggs. I get them from my pal who raises chickens. I can't eat Winn Dixie eggs—if you grew up like some of us did, then you'll know supermarket eggs taste a lot like toddler snot.

She's off work the next few days, it feels like a long weekend. She'll stay in her pajamas, and I'll putter around. We don't say much around the house.

"You hear about Sister So-And-So getting married?" I might say.

"Yep," she'll remark. "Her new husband is a real piece of..."

You get the idea.

She might watch murder mysteries on the sofa. Or: wander into my office while I'm working. She'll tell me she's unsure of what we're having for supper. And we will discuss this subject at least forty times per day.

"You want pizza tonight?" I'll ask.

"No, I wanna eat at home," she'll say.

"Fine, but I don't want beans again, I'm sick of beans."

And then I get a black eye.

My friend died last week. It happened in his car, in a parking lot. They found him sitting in the front seat with a to-go box on his lap. Nobody saw it coming. A heart attack.

He sat there a full day until his car idled itself out of gas. He was a good man with a nice wife. No kids. We drank together some. I called him my cousin, he called me, Red.

His wife told me, "Our house feels empty now. I miss little things that I never paid attention to. I've been eating breakfast alone all week. That's hard."

Look, I'm no dummy. I know one day the one who sleeps beside me will kick the oxygen habit. Or maybe it'll be me who goes first. God. I don't want to think about it.

Still, I can't help but believe that ambition doesn't amount to a hill of beans in this life. Neither does money, or whatever-the-hell else it is people get so lost looking for.

Honey, if you're reading this, I'm not writing to say I love you—though God knows, I do.

It's more than that.

I love eating breakfast with you.

ROLE MODELS

My uncle was always broke. After my father died, he'd take me into town and say, "I forgot my money-clip, how much you got?"

I'd reach in my pocket and give him what pittance I had. He'd smile. "Thank God, I was afraid we wouldn't have gas to get home."

He sunk his little bit of savings into a rusted Dodge RV that was hardly bolted together. Whenever the thing came bounding down our road, it sounded like a shopping cart.

The door was loose, one window was covered with cardboard. Inside: a couch he'd found on the side of the road which used to smell like cat urine.

He parked in our cattle pasture. The cows took to him quicker than they ever took to me. They wandered around his vehicle and looked through his windows.

Often, I'd find him in a lawn chair outside, with two Aberdeens underneath his awning. He'd named the red one, Barbara. Whenever he'd see me coming to visit, he'd slap her hindparts, saying, "Get outta here old girl, make room for my nephew."

Barbara complained.

I'd sit with him half the day sometimes. He was lonely, I was fatherless. Some friendships are meant to be.

He told stories—he has millions. I could pass entire afternoons listening to one after another. Whenever he'd tell a blatant false one, he'd raise his hand and say, "Hundred and twenty percent true. Ain't that right, Barbara?"

Barbara didn't like being brought into disputes.

My uncle was, by all means, a decided failure. Not the kind of example many people aspire to become. He worked in a lowly fertilizer plant, smelled bad, and couldn't afford supper. And, he was the only living member of my family lazy enough to pick guitar, or memorize dirty jokes.

To me, he was a genius.

You should've heard his knockout storytelling. Sometimes, he'd talk until one in the morning—until I'd laugh so hard I peed. Or: he'd play guitar for his nephew, who didn't want to go to bed because he missed his father.

And it was he who once told me, "You don't wanna be like me. Sure, you can learn a few of my stories, or maybe play music like me. But make better of your life than I did. You don't wanna be a damn loser."

Anyway, as it happens I don't know much about anything. And I know less about successful adulthood. But, if storytelling, music, and giving love to a child who hurts inside makes someone a loser.

The world could use a lot more of them.

Happy birthday, Uncle.

A FEW GOOD MEN

There's a portrait in my friend's office. An eight-year-old drew it. My friend's ears look like wide-open car doors, but otherwise I'd say it's an undoubtedly accurate depiction.

My friend teaches art. Well, sort of. He teaches it once every two months, since Alabama schools have deemphasized arts and music. He tells me his students didn't even know how to operate scissors or draw basic happy faces.

"It's sad," he says. "Technology has changed everything. And so has the school system, we've just kinda let art dry up."

Most of his students spend school hours doing math homework.

"If our school doesn't bring math grades up," my friend says. "It affects our funding. These kids have an hour of homework every night. It's crazy. There's no time for kids to go outside and play anymore."

God help me.

I don't have many bones to pick with the society. In fact, I believe American kids are quite privileged. Furthermore, my wife is a math teacher, so I need to be careful or I'll be sleeping in the barn. But it burdens me to think children don't have time to practice shooting cap guns.

My friend decided to fix this by holding after-school art classes.

"It was just me and a few other dads," he said. "The first class, we taught'em to draw turtle shells. Which is just a bunch of equilateral octagons."

For the love of Crayola, refrain from the math jargon.

"Kids got into it," he went on. "Then, we taught'em faces. Everyone took turns drawing portraits of their partners."

His art class grew.

Soon, several kids and parents stayed after school to get messy with paint and clay. Once, they even made guitars out of cigar boxes.

And then the county got involved. Someone didn't like the idea of folks on school property without sufficient staff. After all, someone could get injured with a paintbrush on school grounds.

One parent suggested hiring personnel to stay after school. The county said it would cost too much. So they shut the art class down.

"I was bummed at first," he said. "But then I decided, it was our mission to make sure kids had something else to do besides homework, you know, to keep their minds stimulated."

So, he found a local church who agreed to help. Not only did they host the program, they donated all art supplies, too.

"These're different times," said my friend. "Kids need us. If we're not fighting for the happiness of our kids, what'n the hell are we fighting for?"

I wish I could follow that line up.

But I can't.

TWO GROWING BOYS

Cheeseburgers are God's gift to humanity. You can quote me on that. Once, I traveled to Montgomery, to try what some call Alabama's best burger—at a hole-in-the-wall place called Vicki's Lunch Van.

As it happens, Vicki's is not a van. It's an old building. Furthermore, I can assure you, the rumors are false. This is not Alabama's best. This is the best in the cotton-picking United States.

Anyway, I'm getting ahead of myself.

Long ago, when I worked as a house framer, I ate burgers every lunch. This went on for years. I ordered them with extra cheese and pickles.

My friend ate with me. He had a curly black afro and stuttered badly. Because of this, he usually wanted me to order for him. So, each day at lunchtime, I'd tell the girl at the counter, "Two burgers, fixed pretty." She knew what to do.

We'd eat on the tailgate. My buddy would often say something like, "Y-y-you think you could g-g-get me more C-C-Coke?"

"What am I, your butler?" I'd say, then I'd get him a refill.

I remember the day he told me about a girl.

He said they'd gone bowling. And then, with great

enthusiasm, he explained how she was a special girl. She had a young son, with cystic fibrosis. She lived with her friend in a bad part of town. Their relationship was, for all practical purposes, fiscal failure. Between them, all they had were a few nickels and a car payment.

He married her.

I showed up for the wedding. There were maybe five people attending. His mother, brother, and a few others who looked like they'd just gotten off work. His tux was cheap, so was her dress. Her son sat in the front row, crutches on his lap.

When my friend said his vows, he stammered so hard the preacher winced. His bride never quit smiling.

They moved out of town—she wanted to be closer to her mother, since raising her son was a handful. The whole thing happened fast, he hardly knew what hit him. After a few weeks, I was eating lunches all by myself.

I saw him yesterday.

Of all places, he was in the supermarket. He was with his family, visiting town for the weekend. His wife was just as beautiful as ever. His son: huge, and walking without crutches. My pal is happy.

"This woman is my angel," he said, with no stammer. "Before her, I didn't believe love was real."

He and I hugged. I embraced him a little longer than you're supposed to. Maybe I even got a little misty, I can't really remember. I glanced in his cart.

Thank God.

He still eats ground beef.

YOU

Pinch yourself. Right now. Go ahead. I'll wait.

You feel that? You are—to put this quite bluntly—pretty damn incredible. If you don't believe me, think back to when you used to poop your diaper five times per day. You've come a long way since then, big guy. Your brain is faster, your skin tougher, you don't make impulsive decisions, you'll even admit when you're wrong.

And.

You're getting better looking with age. Hand to God. If you think I'm making this up, go look at your prom pictures. Better yet, try taking cellphone photos of yourself. Just be certain you hold the camera above you when you do it. Otherwise, your face will turn out looking like Porky Pig's older cousin.

Look, I don't care if you have wrinkles on your forehead and silver in your hair. Who ever said this was a bad thing? Not me. Because I squarely disagree. I love gray hair, and I think wrinkles are privileges some people never get. Besides, I'd rather have crow's feet and good insurance, than the body of a sixteen-year-old who couldn't get heartburn even if he ate Cajun-sausage pizza past five o'clock.

Each year, month, week, day, hour, minute, second,

you get better and better. And every few seasons, you make new friends—they all think you're wonderful. I know this, because I'm one of them.

Furthermore, if you keep making buddies at this rate, by the time you take the ferry to Beulah Land, you'll have your own personal ethnic group.

Also,—and try to stay with me here—you look good naked.

I just lost most of you. But I'm not sorry. I've never seen you naked, thank God, but you have. And I hope you stand before a mirror, jaybird-style, admiring the body God gave you. I don't care what shape it is. It's perfect.

If you're a woman, you ought to take pride in your hips—no matter their circumference—and your other attributes, too. If you're a man, smack that hair-covered beer belly and revel in its jiggle, hoss. It took a lot of suds to make that thing. This is your body. Damn the man who tells you there's something wrong with it.

I don't care what magazines say, reality television, pop musicians, high school bullies, ex-boyfriends, ex-girlfriends, judgmental parents, disgruntled minimum-wage managers, or anyone else. You are effulgently spectacular—and I don't even know what that word means.

This is YOU we're talking about. You're the best thing some people have ever seen. The kindest, gentlest, most loyal, beautiful, thoughtful, genuine, alive, and selfless creature anyone in this universe ever had the pleasure of knowing.

And if that's not the case...

You still have time.

ANGELS AND MEN

We went to college together. He worked at a hardware store. His parents were illegal immigrants who didn't speak a lick of English. He was born in Prattville, but spoke with a Latino accent.

His high school counselor helped him choose a career path. He joined the Marines, got a few tattoos, served his country, then enrolled in college on the GI bill. Today, he has a wife, two children, and he's an engineer. He cares for both elderly parents.

He told me once, "My father come to this country so I have opportunities. Taking care of them is the least I can do."

She was pretty, but she always looked tired. You would too if you worked three jobs. Two waitress jobs. One cleaning hotel rooms.

Her sister was sick. Bedridden. When my friend wasn't cleaning rooms or bussing tables, she was swapping shifts with her mother to care for her.

When her sister finally passed, she told me, "I wish I could'a done more for her."

More.

His parents were drug dealers. They were rough customers. As a five-year-old, he spent one year living in a tent before they got arrested. When they were hauled off to prison, his grandparents gained custody of him.

Suddenly, he had his own room. A television. He watched all the Westerns he could stand. When he got older, he decided to try his hand at junior calf riding, and team roping. He was awful. Anyway, he's a school teacher now.

He saw his father recently, he treated him to breakfast. His father told him, "After all I put you through, I want you to know I'm proud'a you."

His father overdosed a few months thereafter.

She's been married forty-eight years now. Twelve years ago, her husband's tremors started. It was Parkinson's. Today, he can't get a spoon to his mouth, or walk without help. He's in diapers. She is his caregiver.

She tells me, "My life is rewarding, but it's hellish work."

Hellish, but noble.

Yesterday, I had lunch with a friend. He tells me he's a workaholic, hellbent on climbing a corporate ladder. He's proud of himself. He's got a summer home and a car that costs more than my liver. But he's unhappy. He's had three wives already. He says all three heartaches were their fault because,—in his own words—"everyone is so frickin' selfish."

I'm sorry that's been his experience. God knows, there are lost souls in the world who would slice your throat just to get ahead.

Even so, until they bury me, I'll keep believing those folks are outnumbered.

By caregivers.

MY COUNTRY 'TIS OF THEE

The day the planes hit the towers in New York was my late father's birthday. I was at work. Ten of us stood on a job site, hands resting on toolbelts, sweating like hogs, listening to a radio the size of a rice box.

The commentator announced: "America is doomed, folks."

Doomed.

Five fellas cut work early. One foreman called his sister in Manhattan. The rest of us just looked for atomic mushroom clouds.

The next day: I counted four hundred American flags hanging from every nook and cranny of our world. At our construction site, we hung a two-story flag. My friend even got a flag tattoo on his ankle.

I'm not going to mince words. I love this land. You want to know why?

I thought you'd never ask.

The Everglades at sunrise, there's the first reason.

Alabama football. There's number two.

Furthermore: I've been fortunate enough to do a few patriotic things in my day. Like baling hay in middle Alabama. Or: shooting a coon in south Georgia—then eating the god-forsaken thing with ketchup.

I've seen the Oak Ridge Boys sing "Elvira," and Mel

Tillis sing "Coca-Cola Cowboy." I've changed a tire on an Oklahoma highway. I've raised leghorns, and wrung more red-rock necks than I can shake a wishbone at.

I've camped inside the Grand Canyon, and shaken hands with Mickey Mouse in Orlando. I've watched Steel Magnolias nearly seven thousand times.

I've eaten pozole prepared by a Mexican family who lived in the woods. I worked one summer on a cattle farm—and slept under the stars after a full day tagging heifer ears. I've fished in the Gulf of Mexico, seen two tornadoes, and washed my drawers in the Mississippi River.

I've worked in an ice cream shop—and gained fourteen pounds. I've staked heirlooms, boiled peanuts, eaten homemade biscuits, and drank bathtub moonshine. I can eat a full jar of peanut butter. I've pulled over for automobile funeral processions, and been part of a few.

I've heard a man pray in tongues at a funeral, I've attended exactly one Junior League meeting, and I have been inebriated at the Iron Bowl.

I've watched Willie Nelson sing, "America the Beautiful," I've eaten Conecuh sausage, and I've shot bottle rockets on the Fourth of July.

I own fifty pairs of Levi 501's, drink warm beer from a can, have mediocre health insurance, and I'd rather waste money on a baseball game than a cruise to Greece.

My roughneck father was born on the eleventh day of September. My ancestors are blue-collar nothings. Just like me. I'm a nobody. I haven't done anything remotely noteworthy, and most likely, you don't even know who I am.

But I'm American.

And I'm proud as hell about it.

FRIENDS

The moment I first heard of my father's death, I wanted to run. I don't know why. It was a gut instinct. I wanted to dart out the door, past ponds, down dirt roads, into the creek-bed, and keep going until I hit Baton Rouge.

I flew toward the door, but didn't unbolt it fast enough. They caught me while I flailed like an idiot. A room of people watched while I cried.

It wasn't supposed to happen that way. I wasn't supposed to feel so naked, with so many gawkers. But that's the way it happens.

The following days were black. I cried myself to sleep. I couldn't eat. I looked in our kitchen and saw more casserole dishes than I'd seen in my cotton-picking life. I tried to eat chicken and dumplings, but couldn't keep them down. I ended up vomiting in the sink.

There was a live oak, at the edge of our pasture, behind the cattle fence. I went there to be alone, my Labrador followed me.

She and I passed entire days there, until I'd fall asleep with her on my lap. Sometimes I didn't get back until well after dark.

Once, I even fell asleep in the shower. The water turned ice-cold and I realized I'd been out for nearly thirty minutes.

Nobody tells you grief feels a lot like exhaustion. It's demoralizing, and reshapes your mind. During the nighttime, you feel afraid. In the days, you wonder why the sun seems so dim. You still want to run, but you don't know where to go, or why.

Food tastes bad. Conversations feel shallow. Your friends seem selfish and disinterested. And whenever you remember your loved one, you hope it will bring relief. It doesn't. It slices like sheet metal.

Why am I telling you this?

Because two out of two people die. One day, you're going to go through this—if you don't die first. Chances are you've already endured it.

The sharp pain lasts for a long time, until one day it feels like a bruise. One day, the time you spent sleeping in cattle pastures seems like faded memories. Mornings are brighter. People, nature, and food are more important than before.

It happened so slow you hardly realized it. Then, you look at the calendar and remember how long it's been. You think of how much you've learned. Like: how good it feels to pet dogs, sit on porches, or play Scrabble. Or: how human life seems to last about as long as a six-pack.

Anyway, I don't know who you are, friend. But I want you to know that you'll smile again.

When that finally happens, drop me a line.

Because I'm praying for you.

'BAMA DIRT

"He was a dirt farmer, last of his kind," she said. "Poor as a church mouse, we never had money."

Back then, few Alabama farms did. After a Depression, a world war, and losing acres of cotton to the boll weevil, she says they were almost licked. Then he started growing tobacco.

"His daddy was a cripple," she said. "Not only did we farm, we cared for my husband's daddy, fed him meals, bathed him."

When her husband wasn't doing that, he was supervising seven field workers. Or maybe it was ten. She can't remember.

"He was good to'em," she went on. "Remember once, this little old man came running and said, 'My wife's sick, boss. Think she's dying.' Right in the middle of a work day, they took her to the hospital. My husband paid for everything, even her funeral. It was sad."

But farming wasn't all sadness and poverty, there were high moments, too.

"Tobacco's gotten a bad name over the years, but we thanked God for the money. I used to string leaves with the women all day, we sang work songs, you wanna hear one?"

Why not.

She hummed a somber melody, tapping her fingers to keep rhythm. Her voice was old, but if you listened close enough, you heard the entire South.

"When the crops got sold, we'd throw parties. Folks came from everywhere. Black, white, all kinds, didn't matter. We ate and drank until the sun came up."

She laughed.

"Thing about farmers is, they work twice as hard for half as much. My kids're surprised when I tell'em how poor we were. 'Course everyone was poor then. But, we never got so down we lost our morals."

God forbid.

These were decent men, with good values. Men like her husband. Who paid workers before himself, who bought them new clothes and shoes. Who attended their baby dedications, hat in hand.

He was one of the men you won't read about in history textbooks, even though their faces ought to be on the covers. A man who was above nothing, beneath no one.

Who slaughtered his own hogs, sweat in his own fields, sharpened his own tools, and still had time to kiss his kids goodnight. Who ate family suppers, doled out whippings, darned his own socks, and birthed his own son in the living room when the doctor was out of town.

"When he died," she said. "It kinda felt like a whole generation went with him. He was a good man."

But as it happens, she made a grave understatement. He was more than good.

He was a farmer.

FAMOUS GIRL

She almost wouldn't let me write about her. She finally agreed, but only after I vowed to cut her lawn. That's no joke.

First, I had to promise I wouldn't give away much information about her identity. Then, I had to edge her sidewalk.

Her lawn-man had bronchitis.

"Well," she said. "As a little girl I wanted to be famous. I wanted see something big, to get out of a small town and see stuff. I used to clip out pictures of exotic places and hang them in my room."

She's silver-haired now, her left hip is a wreck, but she has terrific posture. And she looks stately in her pearls.

As it happened, fame wasn't so hard to accomplish. She studied hard, attended college, then found a job selling makeup on television. There, she married a man. He wanted notoriety too. To be a politician.

Which is like fame, only filthier.

Before she knew it, she was traveling back and forth, shaking the right hands, kissing babies, mumbling inspiring things.

"He started off a good man," she said. "Wanted to change things. In the sixties, he had ideas for water-treatment that would've changed everything. He was, 'green,' before there was such a word. Fought for equality, too."

But ideals don't last in politics. They're like candlesticks in a hurricane.

"Everyone shot him down," she went on. "Too many people offered him too much money to push bad ideas. So, one day, I think he just started playing their game."

They went to parties, she wore white gloves. They ate at fancy restaurants, she used the right forks. They rode convertibles in parades, she waved to crowds. They slept in separate bedrooms—sometimes his secretaries spent nights in his.

She faded inside.

"I don't think people know what goes on in that world. It's a crooked way to make a living. It's worse now. I remember when he and his buddy..."

Let's call his buddy an esteemed official.

"...flew to Ireland one afternoon just to play golf for a few hours. Taxpayers paid for the whole thing. And that's the sweetest-smelling story I can think of. I have stories about prostitutes that'd make you sick."

No thanks, ma'am. I'm Southern Baptist.

After years of watching his morals spiral, she left him. She took her two children and moved to the town where she was born. She started over. She even planted a garden out back.

No more dinner parties.

"I'm sorry I ever wanted to leave this place," she says, pointing through her back window. "It was greed for more that ruined us. I'm happy now."

I asked who she was voting for in the upcoming elections. She told me she quit voting forty years ago, since she knew too many of the politicians personally. I asked her to share a few views.

She laughed.

ON THE ROAD WITH SEAN OF THE SOUTH

"Honey," she said. "I never discuss politics with anyone but the Good Lord."

And then I push-mowed her grass.

COOKIES

I was going to write about something else, but then a stranger dropped homemade cookies onto my front porch. It was the same woman who said, "Don't trust a baker who looks good in a two-piece."

It took me a few hours to understand that. By then, I'd finished the cookies.

There was a note attached. She wrote: "I make everything the right way."

Well, heaven bless the good woman who does not walk in the path of the unrighteous, nor practice the spiritual defamation of plastic-tubed biscuits and frozen breakfast burritos.

I'd like the record to show that I miss the days of real food . I miss country ham—the kind that comes from a hog in a nearby county. And real fried chicken—made with an iron skillet and slippery floor.

Last Christmas, a friend served ham from Walmart. It was an affront to decency. The meal tasted like undercooked linoleum. The package label on the ham read: China. I'd rather eat chicken feet than red ham.

Not only that.

I miss grits that come from feed-sacks, that take more than two minutes to prepare. I miss French fries cut before frying. I miss popcorn made in a skillet, with enough butter to short circuit U.S. Congress.

A friend made microwave popcorn during a football game last weekend. When it finished popping, he opened a yellow packet of slime, labeled, "butter-flavored topping." That gold-colored degradation ruined my favorite shirt.

And my mouth.

What happened to real butter? The kind that made your arm muscles sore. Or ice cream that turned into soup if you didn't eat it quick. Commercial ice cream wouldn't melt on my dashboard.

I'm just getting warmed up.

I miss how it was before people worried about deadly mosquito bites, dookie in our drinking water, whole milk, and deer ticks. As a boy, deer ticks were no cause for national alarm. Now they'll turn your brain into butter-flavored industrial pump lubricant.

Anyway, what I'm driving at is:

I met a man who went fishing with his nine-year-old son. While on shore, he saw a deputy in a khaki uniform. My pal knew something was wrong. The deputy inspected the fish his son caught, then asked to see fishing licenses.

My friend, like any self-respecting Southerner, did not have a license, nor has he ever. Johnny Policeman fined him. His son had to throw his fish back. And the deputy called his mama ugly.

Mother of fatback.

I don't know how to get things back to the way they were—back when a grit was a grit. But, I wish it could be done. God help me, I do. Not because I'm not happy, but because the world doesn't seem happy.

Thanks for these sugar cookies, ma'am.

And God bless the good woman who wears a one-piece.

ELDERS

His era is gone. He knows that. His barefoot childhood is just a memory. The soles of his young feet were like maple. He could walk five miles on those dogs. Today, children wear shoes with lights in them.

Something else about him:

He made fishing rods out of cane stalks. They weren't like store-bought varieties—they were better. In the afternoons, he'd steal corn from nearby fields, eat it raw, then puff a pipeful of fresh-picked rabbit tobacco.

If you ask me, it sounds like a shoeless fairytale. But it's not. It's lower Alabama.

He spent enough time on the Conecuh to be part catfish. In fact, it's where he took his wife for their honeymoon. She loves him. They get along.

He took up chewing twist tobacco. Nowadays, he has to special order it. Nobody sells twist anymore. It's a bad habit. At first chewing was something he did infrequently. Then it turned into routine. Now, he couldn't tell a story without it.

And stories. He spins good ones.

You want comedies? He'll tell you about when he let a raccoon loose during a revival meeting—eons before they wrote country songs about it. You want mysteries? He'll tell you about the harlot found dead in a wealthy man's living room. Dramas? The one about his cousin—who fell in love with his own sister.

Anyway, the old fella has a television. A big one. His kids bought it for his birthday. But it's still wrapped in a box on the guest bed. He doesn't want it.

"He used to watch some TV," his wife said. "Sunday movies, or football, he don't no more. Sometimes he listens to football on the radio."

Ask him what's going on in the world. He'll tell you about the weather, where So-And-So's boy goes to college, about the deer the McWhoevers shot last weekend. He doesn't know what the Zika virus is, doesn't care who the Kardashians are. He's too busy piddling in his workshop, spitting in old coffee cans.

He's got his share of medical issues. He has back problems, he can't hear worth a Shinola, he chews too much, and he's got arthritis in both feet.

The world doesn't seem to care much for its elders. It's a shame. This was their world once—before we came along and put blinking lights in our tennis shoes.

But if you sit with an old soul for a while, you might find time slows down. And while they jaw about childhoods and stories they've tucked away, maybe you'll learn something.

Who knows.

Maybe you'll even try going barefoot.

A HOT MESS

She has long pink hair and a ring in her nose. She's only been hairdressing a few years—the money is awful. But she's got a way with folks, and a healthy sense of humor.

"Turn your head to the left," she'll say. "That's good. Now cough for me."

Cute.

There's a photograph tacked to her mirror. In the picture: a heap of kids seated on the steps of an old home, grinning. There are so many in the photo, the picture is busting at the seams.

"That's my family," she says, pointing. "We're a hot mess."

As it happens, only one of the children in the picture is her own—another one came from her husband. The remaining five are adopted.

I ask why she adopted five.

"Fosters," she says. "If you only knew how many kids need homes, breaks your heart." She taps the photo. "See him? His daddy used to beat him with a mop stick before we got him."

That's nothing.

The tallest child's mother overdosed in a public park —they found him sleeping in a twisty-slide. The two black sisters: rescued from a crack house. The little fella with fat cheeks: he has cystic fibrosis and uses crutches.

She didn't mean to adopt them. It just happened.

"Most days," she says. "All I'm doing is running from point A to point B. I want'em to play sports, have friends, but it keeps me busy."

It's hard. Her husband works for the utility company, she cuts hair while the kids are at school. Afterward, she rushes home to make supper and ensure nobody sets the sofa on fire. They're poor as red clay dirt, but they get by.

"Can't remember what it's like to have money," she tells me. "All we do is work. And we just found out I'm pregnant again." She laughs. "I'm three months along."

Congratulations.

When she finishes trimming my hair, she spins me around and says, "Sorry, I feel like I talked your head off. I gotta big mouth."

No you don't. Besides, I like listening. I tipped her as much as I had on me. I wish it'd been more. Then, I asked if I could write about her. The idea surprised her.

"Lord," she says. "Why me?"

Because, ma'am, if the truth be told, I wish I were more like you. In fact, I wish a lot of people were.

"Well," she says. "Reckon if you gonna write something, you're gonna have to send me the link. I'd wanna send it to my mama."

Well, as it turns out, she doesn't have a real mama at all. She has something even better than that.

A foster mother.

ALL THINGS ARE POSSIBLE

Little Sidney Woznicki has spent her life in and out of UAB. She's a solid kid with a will of steel, and a smiling face. She has a bad liver.

When she was a baby, she turned yellow, they knew something was wrong. Doctors did operations. Her mother quit her job—just to manage Sidney's medication list.

Life's been hard. While most eleven-year-olds sit in class, slaving on schoolwork, Sidney prepares for her second liver transplant.

During Sidney's last invasive procedure, her anesthesia didn't work. They say folks heard her screaming from the waiting room.

If there's a tougher little girl out there, I've never seen one.

But you won't find this family complaining, even though their money is disappearing, along with their energy. In fact, according to the Woznickis, "We are so thankful..."

Thankful.

Josh Clem is a Marine. Also tough. He could crawl through acres of mud with a rifle between his teeth. A few months ago, he married Brianna, and since then, they've been glued at the hip.

Last week, on their way home, Josh had to stop the car. His head hurt. They rushed him to the ER. Doctors discovered blood vessels in his brain were rupturing.

Yesterday, surgeons finished a risky brain surgery. Josh is laying in bed right now—Brianna by his side. This has been a long few weeks. Not much sleep, lots of worry.

The couple says they're grateful.

Jasper, Alabama—Mitch Murray is like any crimson-blooded Alabama man. He likes big trucks, football, fishing, and thinks Bear Bryant is a member of the Holy Trinity.

But he's different now.

After a car accident and a brain injury, Mitch can't walk, eat, or talk. To make matters worse, his insurance company dropped him. His wife, Tracy, is perhaps the most hopeful, cotton-picking woman you'll ever meet.

"All things're possible," she says. "I let him know how much I love him, and will always be here for him, I still sit and cry in private. But God has kept him and I am really grateful."

Anyway, why am I telling you all this? You know why. Because this world kicks you in the teeth, then bills you for damages. And after you're bruised, you turn on your television to discover the universe is only seconds away from exploding.

This earth is sick. Mankind is plagued with cosmic atrocities stinking up our solar system, such as: income taxes and politicians. People hate one another. Children starve to death. Families crumble.

I wish I knew how to be grateful—how to find the heaven-sent strength to keep fighting the bad. I'm sorry to say, I don't know how.

But.

I know a little girl who does.

Get well, Sidney

THE GOOD OLD DAYS

The kid behind the bar asked what type of beer I wanted. It was a fancy place, so I asked what kinds they had. It was a mistake. There were nine hundred varieties —not a Budweiser in sight.

The kid handed me an iPad with a menu on the screen.

And before he filled my glass with fifteen-dollar suds, he said, "Sorry, we don't carry Budweiser. This world has changed on you, bucko."

Bucko?

As a matter of fact, you're right, kid. You want to know how much it's changed? My school bus used to drop me two miles from my house after ball practice. Miss Lynn, the driver, refused to go down the hilly dirt roads for fear she'd get stuck. And I don't want to get cliche here, but what I'm saying is: I walked to school, uphill, both ways, on gravel and mud. A lot of us did.

Go ahead, laugh.

In the summers, the canopies of live oaks, and sugar maples covered our roads. I know this because Daddy gave me The Pocket Tree-Encyclopedia. And for each new tree-find, I'd earn a pittance for my piggy bank.

Piggy banks. We had those. They were filled with coins. Anyone below twelve used silver pieces to buy salt peanuts, Coca-Cola, or taffy. Do I sound like a bumpkin yet?

Good.

We got sunburned a lot. We sweat even more. Our shoes wore out, quick. We got poison ivy whenever the wind blew. We plucked so many deer ticks from our bodies we quit counting. Our dogs followed us off-leash, and we've been drinking coffee since before we had armpit hair.

Our girls could ride horses and shoot rifles. We spent weekends loping trails and open fields. There were no smartphones, only baseball, fishing, frog-gigging, and racy jokes. We didn't know about kidney-rotting narcotics, only strawberry moonshine. The worst sins were Red Man chew, unfiltered Camels, necking, and beer.

Beer.

When we were old enough, there were two beers. Miller and Budweiser. If there was a third, it was forty-five minutes away. Whatever was on tap tasted bad, but you learned to like it. Same as you learned to like manual labor, opening doors for ladies, helping strangers change tires, doing dishes, wetting your hair before church, and referring to anyone with a pulse as ma'am or sir.

The kid behind the bar rolled his eyes.

"Gimme a break," he said, playing on his phone. "You're like everyone else, getting all sappy about the good old days."

You bet your app I am, kid. And I'm grateful to be able to. I only hope that one day you talk about your cellphone so fondly.

Thanks for the beer, bucko.

WHITE TRASH

"When you're a kid, you don't know you're white trash," he said. "You don't think about things like that. Hell, I didn't even know we's poor until high school."

Well. Poorness is all relative. He might've had less than the folks living in antebellum estates. But his family was wealthier than, say, most raccoons.

"It finally clicked in my brain," he went on. "Got home from school one day, Daddy said he'd come into a lotta money."

He laughed.

"Turns out, it was only a few-hundred bucks. He strutted like he was a millionaire. Told me he was gonna buy me a new bedroom, since I's sleeping with my little brothers in the same bed."

The next thing his daddy did was drive to Montgomery to a family friend's mobile-home dealership. On the rear lot were rusted single-wides, ready for the dump.

"We walked through'em," my friend said. "Looking for the nicest one, they were disgusting. Rat nests, mildew, just gross."

After selecting a dilapidated single-wide. His daddy's friend let them have it free—only charging a few hundred for towing it.

That same evening, when his daddy got home, he invited his work friends over.

He went on, "Daddy and his buddies got drunk and cut one whole side off our house, with chainsaws, while Mama's in the kitchen fixing supper."

Two nights later, the new trailer arrived. They sandwiched both homes together, connecting them to make a double-wide.

"Having my own room felt like being rich," he said. "I still had no idea it was so trashy until a kid made fun of me at baseball practice. Honestly, I didn't understand what white trash was. Still, it made me cry."

Years went by. He grew up. Moved away. He went to college. He did well for himself. He bought nicer clothes, some dental work. Eventually, he was working a pretty good job, making a decent living.

As a grown man, he visited the same mobile-home dealership as before.

"I was gonna surprise Mama and Daddy with a new trailer. Even put money down on a double-wide. Thought maybe they deserved something slick."

It was a bad idea.

My friend went on, "Daddy got pissed off. He was like: 'Hey, who do you think you are, buying a man a home without asking? I raised you better'n that. Besides, it's my job to help YOU succeed, boy. Not the other way around.'"

My friend took a moment to sniffle. "I realized something. Daddy might've been poor, but he never took hand-outs, and he worked like a dog for us. If he's white trash, maybe that's just how it is."

Well, I see your point.

Except, that daddy of yours ain't trash.

ADOLESCENT PALS

Kids, before I say another word, you should know that I don't give advice—because I don't have any. In fact, I'm still trying to figure out what the hangy thing is in my throat.

But if I DID have advice—which I don't—I'd say this to you, my adolescent pals:

Be who you are.

You might think that's easy. You're wrong. Lots of folks ask you—beg you—to be someone other than you. They don't mean any harm. They've just got deadlines, goals, grand ideas. Or: perhaps they claim to know what's best for you. They don't. You'll have to trust me on that one.

You weren't made to please them.

You were created for everyone—meaning, all mankind. In fact, that's why you're alive. And you aren't any good to humanity if you're pretending to be what some narrow-minded bucket-brain thinks you should be.

How about I say it like this:

I believe everyone is their own sort of animal. Me? I've always been a red squirrel. Squirrels are meant to climb trees, sleep all day, avoid residential dogs, and let all other woodland creatures feed them. It's how we're made.

Squirrels are NOT meant to tow wagons—like pack mules. They aren't meant to swim rivers, burrow in dirt, or fly south for winters. And we're certainly not meant to write. But some of us do.

Anyway, we're squirrels. We have fat cheeks, beady eyes, and poor timing when it comes to oncoming traffic. It would be a crime to pretend we were, say, Labradors. After all, dogs don't climb trees. Just like monkeys don't balance checkbooks. And raccoons can't operate my barbecue grill—even though those little hellions have tried.

Thus, be your own animal. Wear your bright-colored, funky clothes, scribble your name catty-wampus. Wear your silly hat, and don't take it off until Mama says it's time to shower. Love the people you love—also the ones you don't. Be kind. And don't judge adults too harshly, even if we don't understand you.

We adults aren't as smart as we think. Some of us never learned to be ourselves. We have always known we were zebras, turtles, yellowhammers, coonhounds, catfish, gators, or elephants. But we were too busy being jackasses to do anything about it. It's a shame. But it's our problem, not yours.

God made you unique. It might take you a lifetime to figure out what that means. But once you discover it, don't let anyone take it from you.

Remember: this isn't advice, kids. I'm no different than you.

It's just the opinion of an average squirrel.

UNDERDOGS

I see a single mother loading four children into her dilapidated car in the Walmart parking lot. They're pitching a fit, screaming bloody murder.

I'm writing this to her, and to everyone like her.

Also, to the unrecognized, who think they're nothing. People you'll never hear about. The unpopular, unknown, and under-appreciated.

The woman who takes her kids to school early , then cleans motel rooms. The waiter I met at Waffle House—who's been sleeping in a recliner ever since his mother died.

To the man in Piggly Wiggly, helping his eighty-eight-year-old daddy shop.

The blind boy I saw on the beach, who said, "Mama! Listen to that water! It's hypnotizing!"

I closed my eyes and sat at the water's edge for thirty minutes. I'll be damned if that kid wasn't right.

To the lady who feeds animals at the no-kill shelter. She might not be famous, but to the dogs she's a Messiah.

I'm speaking to the man whose wife committed suicide. To Raquel, the rape victim who lives in a halfway house. To the immigrant Mexican boys who pooled money together to buy a bicycle—then gave it to an old man.

To the girl who's pregnant illegitimately, who doesn't know what comes next.

To all underdogs.

To worriers; those who can't stop thinking about money. To the lonely, widows, widowers, orphans, and caregivers.

To the arthritic, the injured, and those who can't remember life without aches.

To addicts, who are clean. To addicts who aren't.

To people who quit believing in Santa. To people who're bad at math. To anyone who likes John Wayne.

To the child I met, who works after school so he can afford food for his little brother. To the girl I know, who decided to be a teacher. To my friend, Charise, who wonders where her dead little girl is.

To you.

You who aren't certain if anyone sees you. Who hopes there's more to life than this. Who lives from smoke-break to smoke-break. Who wonders when your sky is finally going to open up.

You've gone unnoticed long enough.

Today is your cotton-picking day. I hope you don't blush easily, because you're about to get the biggest fanfare this solar system has ever seen. I don't give a cuss if anyone else hears your ovation or not. I hear it. And right now, I'm clapping for you.

And if that single mother should ever read this:

Ma'am, I don't know how it will happen, and I don't know when. But selfish people can only win for so long.

Now it's your turn.

AFTER THE WAR

"My mind ain't what it used to be," she said. "Wish you could'a seen me back then, I was smart."

She's ninety-four. Feisty as a pair of sandy underpants. Southern as ham hocks. Her hands look like prunes, she has a severely bad memory.

But she still remembers when we won the Great War. There aren't many like her left.

"My first son was born during a coastal blackout, in Mobile. Hospital was lit up by candlelight. That's war for you."

She laughed.

"After the war, we felt like we'd triumphed over the Devil. That's when everyone started saying things like, 'I'm proud to be an American,' because we were the good guys."

She may be forgetful, but she's a cheery little thing. More than anyone I've met in a while. And why wouldn't she be? She can vaguely remember the old world. A world which has disappeared—along with console radios, trumpet music, and hamsteaks.

In her fragmented memories, she still attends baking parties—when women sipped tea and cooked all day in farm kitchens.

"Sometimes," she said. "Four or five of us still get together and bake bread and cookies... No. Wait. I don't do that anymore do I?"

She cursed herself.

"Sometimes I get confused."

Anyway, what she means is:

She misses those days. When her kids would play in the barn while she tended kitchen. When she and her husband wandered into town with pocketfuls of change, just to take in a double-feature.

Nowadays, it sounds more like an episode of The Andy Griffith Show. Back then, it was a Thursday.

"Everything was less complicated," she explained. "That's why we were less ugly-acting. Today, folks are miserable. All our kids're sad. Did you know, my granddaughter doesn't even know how to bake. She's too busy."

She scoffed.

"Busy? When I's a girl, we were BUSY baking peach cobblers. Or was it strawberry? No, blackberry."

She's foggy, but she's no less sharp. She's still a lady of her time. And her generation regarded chicken and dumplings as more important than college degrees. Sunshine and grass stains were daily life. Sliced persimmons predicted weather better than Jim Cantore. Breakfasts were twice the size of suppers.

In a way, her broken memory is a kind of blessing. Up there, things are still uncomplicated and easy.

"Things were so simple back then," she said. "Maybe it was simpleness that kept us so happy. You know, happiness ain't always about being happy. Sometimes it's about not complaining."

I looked up from my notepad. I asked if she'd repeat that last gem of advice.

As it happened, she'd already forgotten what she'd said.

But it doesn't matter.

Because I don't think I ever will.

TO BE IN LOVE

They were married a long time. Sixty-seven years to be exact.

My friend's daddy had a voice like a tuba, and a drawl as thick as sorghum syrup. The man was as tall as a pine, and about as skinny, too.

When he met her, she was an eighteen-year-old, non-English-speaking Mexican. His daddy: just out of the Army—without any idea of what he wanted in life.

Fate happened on the day my friend's father saw some hoodlums harassing a Mexican girl and her two young sisters, outside a cafe in Atlanta. The men made horrible gestures toward the girls. My friend's father intervened and got his hindparts whooped. The fight broke his ribs, but he claimed the girl's brown eyes were worth it.

Theirs was an ill-conceived relationship. Not only did both families oppose the marriage, but neither of the lovebirds spoke the other's language. They were as different as it got.

So, they eloped.

Eventually, they learned how to speak to one another. It took years of practice. Whenever they'd visit her family, his daddy tried his best to speak a fragmented Spanish.

According to my friend, his childhood home was a loving one—with good chicharrones.

In his mother's elderly years, she came down with headaches. Bad ones. My friend said the torment would linger for days. He said his daddy would lay beside her on the bed in a dark room. And, since small noises pained her, his father would just listen to her breathe, his ear against her chest.

"My parents were in love," my friend says. "I used to think everyone's parents were like that. But I know that's not how it goes .

"When my mama got sick, it was like someone was killing Daddy from the inside out. That's when his Parkinson's got real bad."

My friend's mother suffered so long that when she passed it was a blessing. But his father wasn't the same afterward. In fact, he was so affected, he wouldn't even speak about his late wife. To him, it felt profane to use her name.

But it didn't matter. As it turned out, his daddy would only live two hundred days after his mother's funeral.

And when the old man finally left this world, they say he smiled, saying, "Today is the day I get to see my Gabriella."

Then he mumbled something in broken Spanish, and his eyes rolled back into his head.

Anyway, maybe you don't believe in real love. After all, a lot of people don't. Some folks think the idea of this kind of love is just a well-thought-up myth, suited more for fairytales than daily life.

Well.

Those people are wrong.

ALL THE TINY TREES

I'm in a pecan orchard. The trees are blocking out the sun, and I'm in some kind of heaven. Pecan trees do that to me. I could spend an entire day here.

The year before my father died, we planted nearly one-acre's-worth of baby pecans.

I'll bet they're huge now.

It was late October, chilly weather. We dug holes all day. I wore a coonskin cap made from real raccoon. My father hand-made the thing when he was a young man. Folks from our pedigree often hunt coons with spotlights and longneck bottles on the weekends.

While planting each tree-row, he blasted music from his truck cab. I can't remember which songs were playing, all I remember was a twang.

While we worked, Don followed us around.

Don was a duck. He was pure white, and behaved cantankerously toward anyone but Daddy. The old bird hung around wherever Daddy went. Sometimes, you'd see them walking the fence posts, side by side.

"Don," he'd sometimes say. "Why don't you make yourself useful, dammit?"

Don would just stand there, blinking.

"You freeloader," he'd go on, "I'm gonna eat you if you don't start pulling your weight."

But Daddy would've never done such a thing. He didn't want to admit that he loved that stupid bird. He did. Later that year, we found Don's white feathers scattered all over the yard, I saw Daddy cry.

After we'd finished planting the trees, we looked at the mini-orchard in the low sun. Daddy let me sip his beer. Don wandered back and forth, grunting.

The pecans sat in long rows, straight and neat. Like a little army.

"One day," said Daddy. "Maybe these things'll make a little money."

I was too tired to care whether they ever would. We'd worked so hard, I was half-delirious.

Daddy finally looked at me and said, "These trees'll outlive me. One day, they'll be huge. Hell, maybe I'll see'em from heaven, and be proud that you and me planted them."

I didn't know how to answer him, so I just nodded.

Truth told, I don't know why I'm telling you this. Maybe these pecans are getting to me.

But it's been a long time since my father died. When he passed, he left me alone, and it seemed like the world quit spinning. I suppose, when I look at these trees, I think about that. I think of who I am, wondering who I've grown up to be.

And I hope he sees me.

I still have that coon hat.

SOUTHERN MOON

If you ever park in a South Alabama field at night, you'll see things that take your breath away. The big waves of grass make it seem as though you're in the middle of creation.

And God, these stars.

If you happen to know a place like this, don't tell anyone where it is, or else they'll build a shopping mall on it.

Of course, at this hour, it's not about the field, really. It's about the moon.

I'm writing this while sitting in my truck. I've just spent the last three hours watching the moon. Ellie Mae, my coonhound is with me. We split a hamburger for supper on the tailgate—though not equally. She ate the beef, I ate the bread.

Rotten dog.

When she was done, she stared upward at the sky. She held her eyes on the moon like she could see Neil Armstrong. She stayed like that twenty minutes.

I've never seen a dog do that before.

You know, I'm lucky. Admittedly, I haven't seen much in my life, and I haven't visited anywhere of merit. But I'm lucky just the same. And I'd be hard pressed to get any more satisfied than I am right now.

Yeah, I know, life is hard. And they say being happy is even harder. It's true. I've known heartache. So have you.

The world can be mean. Some days you wake up and someone busts you in the teeth before it's even lunchtime. It's easy to get sad.

But don't stay that way. You can take my word for it: it will ruin you.

Besides, look at this field. Look at this moon. This world isn't all thorns. It's a nice place. We have hamburgers, Ford trucks, coonhounds, number-one pencils, Saturday-morning cartoons, and teenage romances.

I love to watch teenage lovebirds hold hands, something about it makes me believe in love.

I once saw a boy and girl in the movie theater. They might've been fourteen. They sat in front of me. The boy's nervousness could've filled a dump truck. When he finally put his arm around the girl, we exchanged glances. He smiled. I winked. I don't even remember which movie it was.

I doubt that kid does, either.

Anyway, you don't know me from Adam's house cat, but it doesn't matter. You're just like I am. You put one shoe on at a time. You've been wounded, lied to, abused, fired, rejected, or fallen victim to the horrors of American politics. Either way, it's left you feeling alone.

Well, just take a gander at this moon. It's been making appearances every night since the dawn of man.

And it comes out each evening just to tell you one thing:

You are not alone.

And never have been.

MAN WITH A TRUCK

"I love this country," he said. "Seen every inch of it. Been driving a truck forty-three years."

He's old. Lines all over his face. Tall. He's wearing a turquoise belt buckle, faded Wranglers, and steel-toed boots. He's making a delivery in North Carolina tomorrow. He's hoping to see the mountains before the sun goes down.

"I's raised a ways outside Shreveport," he went on. "Town so small, we went to kindergarten barefoot, sometimes. Seems like forever ago. I signed up for the Marines soon as I could, wanted to see the world."

His was a short-lived military career. A patrol vehicle ran over his back during a mission. It broke his spine. He retired.

"You know," he said. "In the Marines, we got to see how poor other countries were. Some of'em folks is so homeless, they ain't even got a toilet where they can go take a—"

Use your imagination.

He started driving an eighteen-wheeler. The thing cost as much as two houses. He and his wife borrowed the money from a bank to buy the rig.

They saw the entire country.

"Best decision we ever made," he said. "As a driver,

I've racked up seven million log-miles. Maybe seven and a quarter."

If it's out there, he's seen it.

Portland in the fall, Wyoming in the winter, and L.A. at rush hour. He's seen the shadows in the Grand Canyon, driven through the Rockies during storms, and slept on the shoulder in Oklahoma City. He's ridden the highlands of Virginia, and seen every last bit of the Carolinas.

"Took my wife on the road with me," he said. "We was just two Southern hillbillies, but we saw it all. We'd pull over for the night, she'd cook supper, we'd play cards, or just watch the sun go down in the mountains. God, she loved mountains."

She's been gone ten years now. It breaks him up to talk about it.

"Best years of our life," he went on. "When she died, she wanted me to scatter her in the Appalachians. Did you know you have to get a damn permit to do that?"

No, I didn't.

"You know why we liked driving? 'Cause we love this pretty country, driving let us see it. Every night my wife use to pray the Almighty would help folks remember our founding fathers, and how humble they were. She believed in this nation. And no matter how bad it gets, I'll keep believing in it, too."

He stabbed out his cigarette we shook hands, he bid me goodbye.

Chances are, while you're reading this, he's sitting on a sheepskin-covered seat with four-hundred horsepower humming beneath him.

By sunset, he will be in the Appalachians.

And he's bringing fresh cut flowers with him.

DEBATING PEOPLE

I watched the presidential debates in a Pensacola, Florida bar. The man next to me kept shouting at the television, saying, "Oh, for the love of Jeezus!"

Jesus.

The first time I remember hearing that name was when Mrs. Gelding swatted my five-year-old hindparts for telling a certain joke—with a less-than-reputable punchline.

While she beat the whiteness out of my hindcheeks, she hollered, "A little more Jesus never hurt anybody!"

I didn't know who Jesus was. But later, I would learn how fondly Mrs. Gelding felt for him. Rumors claimed she cross-stitched his face onto her cotton britches.

She called him Savior. And this was a revelation. Because until then, I'd understood Roy Rogers held this title.

Over time, I grew to admire Jesus—even though he didn't ride a well-trained horse. You couldn't help but like him, he's famous. Here in the South, you hear about him everywhere. In Tom Thumbs, beauty pageants, billboards, bingo-houses, and beer-joints.

A few nights ago, I drove past a billboard reading: "Jesus will scare the hell out of you."

Then, I turned on the radio and caught the tail end of

a preacher's prayer, which closed with, "...in Jesus' name, amen."

I've even known a man named Jesus. He was Mexican. We worked construction together. On the jobsite, we nicknamed him, Lordy. He was a good sport about it. Sometimes, he'd pretend he could change water into beer.

We'd roll on the floor when he did that.

Jesus once said that his mother gave him the most holy name she could think of. She wanted him to have every chance he could get, since he was born into base poverty. Jesus didn't own shoes until thirteen. At fifteen, he hopped a train for the U.S.

During his time here, he was not treated kindly. If you've ever wanted to know what real hate is, ask Jesus.

Jesus said, "When I was little, my father say, 'Your name come with big burden, chucho. Most loving man who ever lived, was also the most hated.'"

I think about that a lot.

Anyway, I paid my tab and left before the debates ended. They were about as educational as chewing on Energizer batteries.

I'm sorry to say, this world is angrier. People aren't getting nicer. Love is becoming expensive. Hate is free. I believe they'd even crucify Roy Rogers in the town square if he were alive—then hang Trigger out of spite.

I don't care what your religion is. Old Mrs. Gelding was right.

A little more Jesus never hurt anyone.

TOUGH KIDS

He was tough. And poor. I suppose the two go hand in hand sometimes. He grew up fast, without any choice in the matter. Not having money can do that to a child.

We worked together. I didn't know him well—he was too hardened to have any friends. Each morning, he'd show up to my house on a bicycle, I'd give him a ride to the job-site.

When his little brother needed eyeglasses, he took a second job stocking UPS trucks at night. Because of this, he'd show up most days with baggy eyes, sipping a two-liter bottle of Mountain Dew. During lunch, he'd sleep in someone's car until they woke him.

Sometimes, we'd just let him sleep.

He rarely smiled. I don't think anyone ever heard him laugh. And I can't say I blamed him. His mother was a custodian, his sister was a middle-schooler, his father was an inmate, his brothers called him "Daddy."

On his twenty-first birthday, several of us forced him into a Mexican restaurant. It was a miracle he even agreed to come.

But it was a good night. At first, he was uncomfortable. After a few drinks, he loosened up. We laughed, got loud. The waiters put a sombrero on him, they sang happy birthday in broken English. He blushed.

We howled until we went into oxygen debt.

After supper, all the boys stood out front, filling the night air with blue smoke. Nobody said a word to each other, we just exchanged sappy grins—like we were up to no good.

He didn't like our looks. "What's going on, guys?" he finally said.

Nobody moved a muscle.

Then, a dinged up truck came rolling from behind the building, honking its horn. It was junk, but it had a fresh Kelly Green paint-job—the kind done with roller brushes. The front bumper was a bolted-on four-by-four. No tailgate. Broken taillights. The tires were brand new.

He didn't know how to react when we all screamed, "Happy Birthday!" His face stiffened, and he wore the hard glare of a fighter. Not even a blink.

One boy handed over the keys, saying, "It was my dad's truck, hasn't run in years. We got'er going again, fixed'er up, runs good."

No response.

"It's yours," the boy added.

He didn't look like he cared. He only lit another cigarette and pretended as though he were on planet Mars. He was tough to the bitter end.

After all, that's what this world had taught him. Never trust anyone, never get hurt. And never, under any circumstances, let your guard down. He was doing a pretty good job at that.

He noticed our hands were covered in green paint. Then his face split wide open.

We embraced him.

And then he drove straight home and gave the truck to his mother.

CRESTVIEW, FLORIDA

Crestview, Florida—the class of 1966. The tiny group held their fiftieth reunion next door to the police station, at Warrior Hall.

On the front steps, men took swigs from red SOLO cups while smoking cigarettes. Deputies next door, watched and grinned.

I met a woman with white hair. "Know why my hair turned white?" she asked.

Because you love the Lord?

"During senior year," she explained. "We painted, 'seniors of sixty-six' on every surface of this town. By accident, a can of paint spilled on my hair. My friends soaked me in gasoline to get it out. Been gas-blonde ever since."

Looks nice.

That night, I met military vets, lumber salesmen, turkey hunters, tobacco spitters, and lots of other men who like boots better than sneakers. I met a funeral director, a New-York singer, a few drunks, a minister, and a used car salesman.

One man said, "I shouldn't have graduated in sixty-six."

I asked why.

"When I's in third grade, I got held back, 'cause of a

yankee teacher. Couldn't understand nary a word she said. Otherwise, I'd'a graduated in sixty-five."

Yankees.

The catering company rolled out food fit for royalty. Cocktail weenies, tuna salad sandwiches, and congealed salad. People seated themselves at tables and filled the auditorium with laughing.

One man spiked his drink with something from a jelly jar.

"Is that moonshine?" I asked.

"You damn right," he said. "Want some?"

Just two fingers, please.

After supper, they passed around a microphone. Folks told stories. There was the story about when the cheerleaders snuck into the boy's hideout—replacing scandalous magazines with Bibles.

Or: how the seniors used old outhouses as kindling for class bonfires.

There was the time when Sister So-And-So whacked Brother What's-His-Name with a hammer as children—they'll be married fifty years in July.

One fella remembers sneaking out, stealing kisses from his sweetheart before shipping off for Vietnam.

A woman recalls how school buses used to stop for cattle crossings.

Folks talked of how much they miss small-town life. About how things are faster now.

About their kids.

A few already have Parkinson's, one even uses a walker. Some look bad, others look like bombshells. They're still babies, they just don't look like it on the outside anymore.

Their small community has changed. It's grown. They have an Arby's, a Lowe's, a Cracker Barrel. The old haints are gone. Young men don't sip moonshine anymore. But after half a century, everyone here still

agrees, the good old days weren't just good.
They were breathtaking.
And once upon a time, so was Crestview.

OF GRIT AND GIRLS

I'm a survivor is what I am," she says. "I want you to write that in your little article about me."

She's in a chair by the window—a soft recliner. On the table beside her: porcelain figurines of Georgia bulldogs, a few Jesus statues.

"When I's a girl," she says. "I fell off a mule, my hair got caught in the stirrups, thing drug me for half a mile. My daddy said he ain't never seen a tougher girl. Finally ripped my hair clean out."

She's too old to live on her own now, but she still has independence at her retirement facility. Athena comes to help straighten her room now and then. Athena is large, black, kindhearted, and I wish she would consider adopting me.

Athena says, "She don't like to say it, but we think she older than she knows. That's why I thought you'd like writing about her. Think she almost hundred years old, but ain't nobody really sure."

Nobody's sure because she doesn't have a birth certificate.

"I's born in a two-room cabin," the old woman says. "Daddy put me to work plowing the very next day."

Athena laughs at this. She has a beautiful laugh. I wish Athena would let me sit in her lap for a little while.

"Daddy wanted all boys," she goes on. "What he GOT was two girls and two boys. And we were all fine-looking, too."

The girls worked as hard as their brothers, doing chores meant for kids with tough hands and testosterone. By her teenage years, she could plow straight lines and shell peas with her arms tied behind her back. She believes this grit is what helped her survive cancer.

"When I's in my forties," she says. "Doctors found cancer in my breasts, back then all they knew was to cut'em off. They told me I'd probably die anyway."

Athena shakes her head and whispers, "Jesus."

"So, I told'em to cut me. The other treatments made me sick as a dog. I didn't sleep right for five years."

Maybe not. But she's been kicking ever since. And she still settles in front of the television most Saturdays to pull for Georgia.

Her mind moves faster than her mouth. She tells me slowly: "I want anyone who meets me to know they can make it through anything, with faith."

She is more adamant about this than she is about football.

"Oh, she sure do love her football," says Athena. "Only day of the week we let her dip her snuff."

She hears Athena talking about her, so she says again: "Make sure you writes that I'm a SURVIVOR in your article thingy."

Yes ma'am. Survivor.

I surely will.

MY WIFE

She drinks beer with me. That might seem like a little thing to you. It's not. During football season, it's everything. I need a beer-sipping partner when watching games. One who doesn't smell bad or put his feet on my coffee table.

She's smart. I once saw her worm her way out of a traffic violation. She turned on her charm, giggling for the deputy. I sat in the passenger seat, innocent as Helen Keller. The officer kept giving me sideways glances, as though he wanted to say, "C'mon honey, let's ditch the stiff."

She's a Scorpio. Admittedly, I don't know much about zodiacs. But, we get scorpions in our house. And, from what I know about them: (a) you can't kill them, (b) not even with a twelve-gauge.

She's strong. I've seen my wife move a refrigerator by herself. After I had surgery, she muscled the new appliance inside. Then, she cracked open a beer with her teeth, and powdered her nose.

We've traveled the World's Longest Yard Sale a few times—three thousand miles of Southern rust and garbage. I watched her whittle the price on a pair of red cowgirl boots using nothing but her sugary accent. The boots were twenty bucks; she paid a nickel. The man asked for her number. So, she winked and said, "On a scale of one to ten, I'm an eleven."

She can outfish me, outrun me, out-talk, out-argue, and outsmart me. She's slugged me with a baseball bat once—it was an accident. She landed me in the emergency room twice—also accidental. And she has beaten me so hard at Texas Hold'em that I still owe her nearly eight hundred thousand dollars.

She makes chicken soup when I'm sick. I'm talking the real stuff—fresh poultry, plucked clean. Like Mama's. And she can toss together food fit for company using nothing but hominy, butter, and cheese.

And when the doctors told us they found something suspicious growing in her, it felt like a punch to the face. I lost nine pounds over three months, waiting on tests. And when they finally told us it was benign, I felt like I'd been born again.

Today's Saturday. She'll make handmade biscuits, and we'll eat them with Conecuh County sausage. We'll sit on a porch, read the paper, listen to the crickets. I'll go back for seconds. Without her I'm empty. I love her more than my own damn life.

And it might not seem like much to other folks, but when the game comes on, we'll be together.

Drinking cold beer.

WORST WEEK EVER

It was my worst week ever. I had an apartment located smack-dab on the university campus. It smelled like moldy goat cheese. I felt like the oldest student God ever created. Maybe I was.

College kids would point and say things like, "Hey, Grandpa, the morgue's that way."

Then skateboard off.

Anyway, I applied to a school program. The professor said my work stunk. So, I applied to another. I failed the interview. I called my wife.

"What am I doing here?" I said. "The professors treat me like a dumb redneck, students act like I belong in a nursing home."

"You aren't dumb," she said. "But you are kinda redneck."

I persevered—though I was about as uncomfortable as a cricket in a honey puddle. Then, one day, a campus official approached me.

"I don't know how to tell you this," she said. "A computer glitch deleted your name from our system. Sorry, but we have to drop you for several semesters."

"You're kicking me out?" I asked.

"Well, yes."

In a few hours, I was driving back home. I cried in

the truck. I stopped at a gas station, ate three honey buns, and counted the pennies in my pocket to make myself feel worse. My cellphone vibrated. It was my wife.

"It's Daddy," she said, sobbing. "He's fallen. There's a lot of blood. He's in ICU."

When I got home, I forgot all about school. While my wife held vigil at the hospital, I loped into rush-hour traffic for coffee. I considered my future career options, which were less-than plentiful. I was leaning toward taxidermy.

Just then, the vehicle ahead slammed its brakes. I rear-ended it hard. The airbag busted my cheekbone, I went unconscious.

When I awoke in an ambulance, the paramedic wore a grave face. He said, "Good thing you didn't pee your pants, lotta folks mess themselves during car wrecks."

Thank God for small blessings.

In the hospital, Jamie sat beside me. Her father: just down the hall, comatose. I don't recall feeling more despondent than I did that day. In only one week, I'd managed to see my life become an exotic brand of fertilizer.

You're probably wondering why I'm writing something so depressing. Because. Life beats the spit out of you without mercy. And I do believe there's a reason behind it.

Call me nuts, but I don't think your worst moments are coincidences. Take me, for example. If it wasn't for the god-awful, dream-crushing week I just told you about, I'd be miserable, staring at a little gold-framed certificate on my wall. We might not be friends. And you certainly would not be reading this.

Anyway, that was the week my wife said, "You oughta start putting your writing on Facebook."

It was a ridiculous idea.

HIS NAME IS CHRIS

This kid is a busy fella. He's pacing the doctor's waiting room, straightening magazines. I can't figure out why, but he's arranging them into neat stacks, adjusting chairs, too.

He and I are the only ones here. I wish he'd quit fidgeting, he's making me nervous.

He walks up to me. "Can you scoot your chair back a few inches?" he asks.

"My chair?" The truth is, I'm not in the mood to be scooting. My head is about to pop, my chest feels like it's been pumped full of industrial-grade hog snot.

"I'm trying to make this row of chairs STRAIGHT," he says.

"What are you, the janitor?"

No, he's not. His name is Chris. He's skinny, black, and about as tall as a possum standing on its hind legs. I scoot my chair backward and he thanks me.

"I like things to be neat," he's saying.

This kid would have a field day with my office.

While we're talking, I can't hold a cough in any longer. I take a moment to hack up a lung, a rib, and one rusted license plate.

"You're sick," Chris says.

"Yep, bronchitis, here to get a shot and some

antibiotics."

"A shot? I HATE shots."

Wait until you get my age. One day, they quit sticking you in the shoulder and move south.

It turns out, Chris is here with his mother. Her kidneys don't work. She's been withering away the past few years. He says she's lost forty pounds. Treatments aren't helping. And since you can't exactly buy kidneys at Winn Dixie, she's on a long waiting list for a transplant.

According to him, specialists gave her bad news. If they don't get the organ soon, the worst could happen. Chris says people in their church are praying.

"God can do anything," he adds—because Chris is too young to be cynical. "God can probably even make YOU feel better."

Probably, Chris.

He straightens another chair. Then, he sits and hums to himself. His mother finally comes from the back room. He runs to see her. She's young. Skin and bones. Beautiful, but tired-looking.

The receptionist gives him a piece of candy. Chris smiles the same way he would if someone handed him a Heisman Trophy. With a mouthful of chocolate, he says to me, "I hope you feel better."

Then waves goodbye.

God, I know it's been a long time since our last talk. And heaven knows, I'm no saint. I know millions of folks are bending your ear for some important things.

But please.

Help that woman find a kidney.

YOUNG, SOUTHERN, AND PREGNANT

I can't tell you her name. She swore me to secrecy. So, I'm going to call her Patricia. She's an Alabama-born girl, with more brains than a dog has ticks.

Patricia is twenty-three, works full time, goes to college, and she has a seven-year-old son.

"When I got pregnant," Patricia says. "I thought my life was over, you know? Like, I couldn't believe I was having a baby at sixteen. And what was I gonna do with my life?"

It was an adolescent mistake. She tried to hide her growing belly from her mother, but it didn't work. Her mother was no fool. Finally, she sat Patricia down and gave her the third-degree. Patricia hung her head in shame.

"I expected my mom to be disappointed in me, but she wasn't. She was all excited. I was like, 'But Mom, I'm only sixteen.' She just told me, 'Everything's gonna be okay, Patricia. A baby is always a blessing.'"

A blessing.

But as it happened, life's blessings were beginning to run thin. Before Patricia's son was born, her mother died in a head-on collision on the interstate.

"I was messed up," says Patricia. "And it was really scary being by myself at night, thinking I'm gonna have a baby like—alone. I didn't know who to ask for help, so I called my teacher."

Enter Mrs. Murphy: a churchgoing teacher who is as active in her youth group as she is in her classroom. A woman who's as determined as she is smart.

Murphy's first move was to take Patricia to church. The small assembly welcomed the girl with wide-open casserole dishes.

They threw baby showers, took Patricia shopping for new clothes, and if that wasn't enough, Mrs. Murphy scheduled a rotation of women to stay with her at home —nightshift, and dayshift.

"I was never alone," Patricia says. "And when I had my baby, I had like, five or six women in the delivery room with me, cheering me on. I missed my mom so bad."

After the birth, Mrs. Murphy moved in with her. For the first few years she helped raise Patricia's son, and kept young Patricia focused on her schoolwork. According to Patricia, if it hadn't been for Mrs. Murphy, she would've probably given up living.

Patricia is an adult. She's about to graduate college. She's excited—though there is still sadness in her. She misses her mother. But, she has a new family. They're not blood, but they love her no less. And sometimes, it even seems like Patricia's son has a whole handful of mothers.

I asked Patricia what she's majoring in. Without a hesitation, she says, "Oh, I wanna be a teacher."

Well, Patricia, I'd like to point something out, if I may.

You already are, darling.

THE LONG WAY HERE

I took a long drive yesterday. It was accidental. I was only supposed to visit Geneva, Alabama on business. But I got distracted.

Sunshine does that to me.

I practically grew up in a truck bench-seat, taking drives. Daddy and I would pile in and run the roads for no reason. He'd say, "God, calling this weather perfect would be a grave understatement."

Then we'd head for nowhere. We'd chew black licorice, he'd sip a beer can.

Anyway, since I didn't have anything pressing to do, I pointed my truck in whichever direction felt easiest. Ellie Mae laid in the seat beside me—sawing logs.

The scenery: fields, corn rows, pine forests. Bass ponds with cattails on the edges. Pastures green enough to kill.

I stopped at a gas station where I found black licorice. I bought three packs.

One for me, two for Daddy.

More driving. I went for a few hours. It's funny, sometimes the older I get, the more like a child I feel. If you were to call me a responsible adult, you'd be making a grave overstatement.

I passed places like Bellwood, and Clayhatchee. I'll

bet they don't get too worked up in Bellwood.

I ran over the gentle Choctaw. I cruised by an old woman reclining on her porch-sofa, spitting. She waved.

You haven't lived until you've sat on a porch-sofa, swatting the back of your neck.

I drove past junky areas. Clapboard houses, moldy— prettier than new siding could ever be. And overgrown lawns.

Manicured yards make me nervous. Boys can't chase lizards in short grass. And even if they could, why would they?

I zipped past trees as big around as wagon wheels. Rusted trailers. Dilapidated satellite dishes. A broke-down service garage that went belly-up fifty years ago. A church missing its front door.

I came to a four-way stop in the middle of a pasture. It looked like God had hand-drawn a dirt cross in a cotton field. I pulled over. Cranked the windows.

I watched clouds and talked to Daddy. Asked him how he's been getting on.

A police cruiser rolled behind me. He was a friendly fella. He wore no gun on his belt, and enjoyed petting Ellie.

He asked if I was lost.

As it happens, I was. But I was in no hurry to fix it. I was too busy visiting a friend who left me without saying goodbye.

The deputy gave me directions back to the highway, then said, "You enjoy yourself out here. Ain't this weather perfect?"

It was a grave understatement.

Daddy never touched his licorice.

CLASS CLOWN

I don't fit in at grade schools. Truth told, I never have. There's good reason for this:
1. I'm bad at math.
2. That's enough counting.

So here I am, in Mrs. Sylvia's second-grade classroom. I have forty-five minutes with her students. I'm supposed to talk about writing. And Mrs. Sylvia hopes I'll be able to teach them something.

I doubt it.

I don't teach. Once, I trained a Labrador to fetch newspapers. It was a mistake. He spent the rest of his natural life making steaming headlines in our backyard. I told Mrs. Sylvia as much.

Her response: "Look, I don't care WHAT you talk about, just don't let the kids set the building on fire while I'm down the hall."

Thus, we begin class with a simple writing exercise. I give them a fill-in-the-blank sentence, such as: "My mother says I..."

"Stink!" one kid hollers.

"TALK TOO LOUD!" another child adds.

"Hey," says a boy. "I really gotta poop!"

Creative juices are churning, we try another. My next class directive: "Tell me what's most important in your life."

The class runs quiet. Twenty-six towheads reflecting on life-importance, chewing on pencils.

"My most important thing," one kid explains. "Is my brother. He makes me mad, but I love him, he's my BFF."

A girl adds, "People are important."

A redheaded boy chimes in, "I think being happy is most important."

Okay. Happiness. Now you're talking about the Holy Grail of adulthood, kid. Misery is in our drinking water, staying cheery is about as easy as licking a hot skillet.

The truth is, this is a mean world. Every day, mankind thinks up new ways of killing itself. And if it can't succeed, it just taxes people to death. I don't even watch the news without popping Alka-Seltzer.

Opie goes on, "Yeah, but everyone CAN be happy if they love."

"LOVE!" another girl shouts.

Then: a violent bodily noise originating from some poor child's lower digestive tract.

Onslaughts of laughter. Pandemonium breaks out. These kids have lost their cotton-picking minds.

After a few minutes, there is screaming, uninhibited singing, paper-airplanes. If you've ever wondered what real happiness looks like, there's plenty in Mrs. Sylvia's classroom.

When Mrs. Sylvia gets back, students pass in their writing assignments.

One girl hugs my leg and asks me not to leave. Another boy gives me a hand-drawn picture and calls me his hero. A freckled girl loans me a half-eaten Oreo and says she loves me.

"Did you teach'em anything?" Miss Sylvia asks.

Not at all, ma'am.

In fact, I wish I knew half of what they already know.

THIRTEEN AND SERIOUS

I met a boy in the supermarket parking lot. I saw him loading groceries into a rusty car. His young mother sat up front with a baby.

He was a serious kid. Thirteen maybe. His daddy had just died. Brain tumor. It screwed him up.

I helped him load a large bag of dog food. When we finished, he shook my hand like a thirty-year-old.

And for a second, I was thirteen.

In my memory, I'm standing in the gravel parking lot of a rural supermarket. I can hear my kid sister screaming in the truck. Mama soft-talking her.

Behind me: Mister Stew, stepping out of his vehicle. Nosy. He's just learned the news about Daddy. I can see it on his face.

I remember that only a few days earlier, I'd overheard a conversation between two adults—at church. They'd talked about me.

"You hear about his daddy?" one man had remarked.

"No," said the other. "What happened?"

"Kilt his self."

"Oh my God, that kid's gonna be screwed up."

It occurred to me then, that this was my new lot in life. And I would learn this fully when I showed up for ball practice. When all the boys scooted toward the other end of the dugout, avoiding eye-contact.

That day, on the walk home, I tossed my glove into a ditch and never went back.

Even my sleep was cursed. I'd lay awake, unable to shut my eyes for more than a minute. One night, I wandered into our pasture to watch stars. The next morning, Mama found me asleep near the goat pen.

Money got tight. Childhood ended. I learned to do laundry, change lightbulbs, fix sinks. I took thankless jobs. Mama and I pooled our paychecks together for rent. We wore secondhand clothes.

That all seems like a hundred years ago now.

Anyway kid, I don't know what you're feeling. It wouldn't matter if I did. I'm not going to lie, you're going to have your own share of private hell to endure. But either way, I'm asking you to buck up.

Because one day—and you're just going to have to trust me on this—you're going to be a new man. It'll be like God replaced your head with a factory-new model. You'll taste food again, and grass won't look so brown.

And whenever you waltz through a parking lot and see the forlorn face of some poor boy, it'll be your duty to offer him a hand. You won't even have to say a single word.

Just let him know you care.

Because that's what screwed-up people do.

FALLING APART

This place is lousy. The food is awful, the beer comes in plastic cups and tastes like toilet water.

The man beside me at the bar weighs a buck-ten, sopping wet. He has a white handle-bar mustache and old skin that looks like rawhide. If I had to guess his age: one hundred and twelve.

I shouldn't be drinking tonight. I have bronchitis. But I'm a hick, and Alabama's playing Arkansas. I can't do barbecue and football without Budweiser.

"I ain't never seen nothing like it," Mustache says. "Y'all're the luckiest generation, but the MOST miserable."

Miserable. That about describes me right now. I can't quit hacking. My wife had to sleep in the spare bedroom with a pillow over her head last night.

The man goes on, "We got hurricanes, diseases, and people dying, but all we do is fight about politics..."

While he's jawing, I realize that I can't taste my food —or my beer. My tastebuds are collecting unemployment.

Mustache says, "There's so damn much to be grateful for, but folks walk around looking like they been drinking castor oil. You know. Hateful."

I push my sandwich away. The mention of castor oil

has ruined my evening. Mama gave me spoonfuls of the stuff to treat everything from constipation to C-minuses.

"It breaks my heart," Mustache says. "Americans love complaining. It's like they're angry. REALLY angry. Don't know what's happening anymore, we're falling apart from the inside out."

I signal the bartender for my bill, but he's too engrossed with the old man to notice.

The old timer says, "There was a time people were kind. Boys opened doors for girls, folks pulled cars over to help change strangers' tires. If travelers needed shelter, people put them up."

Well, those are sweet thoughts, sir. But that America disappeared along with manual stick-shifts and argyle. Flip on the news, thumb through the paper. This world hates each other.

"What do you think the solution is?" asks the bartender.

The man looks him dead in the eye. He reaches into his wallet and lays two hundred-dollar bills on the counter.

"How about this?" he says, sliding them forward. "How about I do something nice to you? Then—for no reason—you go do something sweet for someone? Dammit. Love. THAT'S how we change America."

The kid pockets the money, smiling. The elderly man shakes my hand and hobbles out of the bar.

When he's gone, the bartender says, "Ain't he something else?"

He was more than that, he was beautiful.

"Beautiful?" The kid belly-laughs. "God, I'll have to tell Daddy you called him that."

THE BIG DAY

They just donated a new piano to the nursing home and rehab where Wanda lives. This is big news for a small place like this. There's a buzz in the air.

Old folks love pianos. They can't help but gather around them. It's instinct.

Wanda says, "A hundred years ago, the only entertainment anyone had was pianos. Mama tried to get me to learn to play, I was too busy running 'round barefoot."

"Me too," said one man. "Spent all my time in the woods, wish I'd learned."

A lady in a wheelchair with Parkinson's adds, "My grandmother was full-blood Cherokee, she hated pianos. A white-man's instrument. Wouldn't let us touch them."

The nurses here know the residents by name, and all day-to-day routines. This is not an easy place to work. One nurse tells me the first time she helped Sister So-And-So use the restroom, it took two hours—she almost resigned. She called it a, "traumatic experience."

"My Paw Paw was a druggist," Wanda went on. "Used to have a piano in his drug store. There was one kid who could flat play. He'd come in and stay all day. All us girls liked him."

The remark is barely noticed by the crowd. They're

too zeroed-in on Rodney—a middle-aged man at the piano. He's the music minister from the Methodist church. Today, he's here to demonstrate the new piano and roll through songs like "Let Us Break Bread Together" or "Amazing Grace."

Wanda and company are waiting.

The nurse comes around and tops everyone's coffee off. She has two pitchers. One with caffeine, the other with brown stink water. How she remembers who gets decaf is beyond me. I ask her how she knows such things.

"It's my job," she tells me. "Been doing it forever. I've known several these residents since I's a kid. Like Miss Amy, she was my kindergarten teacher."

When Rodney begins playing, the world stops spinning. People sing along. Wanda bellows strong enough to knock paint off a fire hydrant. She knows every cotton-picking word to every pea-picking hymn. Another man sits with his eyes closed, he's crying. So are a few others.

It's just music, but to these people, it's something else.

"I've never seen'em so alive," remarks one nurse. "I had no idea it would mean so much."

For two hours, Rodney plays, until he sweat through his shirt. Finally, he takes a break. Wanda leads a standing ovation. Everyone joins in. Even the janitor claps. Rodney looks embarrassed.

"Please," says Rodney, laughing. "You'd think I'd just played for the the Good Lord himself."

You did, Rodney.

Today, he happens to look like a woman named Wanda.

BROTHERS

Whenever Randy was happy, so was his kid brother, Todd. And even though Todd had Down's syndrome, it didn't stop him from being the mirror-image of his idol.

In fact, Todd never knew he was any different than the rest of us. His brother didn't permit such ideas. If anyone even looked at Todd sideways, Randy would tighten his fists.

Sometimes, the two seemed less like brothers and more like one person.

We'd take Randy fishing; Todd came along. We'd go camping; they'd share a tent.

Consequently, one night I felt splattering against the side of my tent, and heard Todd whistling Dixie.

The next morning, Todd said, "Sorry, I thought you were a tree last night."

Still, it was impossible not to like Todd. He laughed hard at jokes, sang loud at campfires, and made simple things seem like privileges.

One summer, Todd got a job on the same construction site his brother worked. He wandered around picking up nails and screws for pocket change. He lost the job when he started playing with a high-powered nail gun—accidentally making pin-cushions out of Randy's truck tires.

Another time: Todd drove his brother to the doctor when he came down with the stomach bug. He piled Randy into the vehicle, fired the engine, and broke the sound barrier.

When the cop pulled him over, Todd instructed the deputy to write him two tickets to save time. The officer was more interested in why Todd was driving without a license—and why he was driving on the median.

But that was long ago. Todd and his brother moved to Tennessee when work slowed down. They grew up, sprouted facial hair. We lost touch. But I still remember the younger versions of them, and how they did everything together.

And I recall the time Todd fell prey to a fistfight because someone called him, "retard." Randy stepped in and ended the rumble in a few seconds. When the scrape was over, Randy told me through bloody lips:

"My dad left us while Todd was still a baby, he called him an ugly freak. He was too stupid to see how great Todd is. Why, he's the thing I love most in this world."

Anyway, a few weeks ago, Randy was on his way home from work and fell asleep at the wheel. I'm sorry to say that it was a dark day in Tennessee.

They tell me Todd gave one hell of a eulogy. And when somebody asked why he wasn't crying, he answered:

"Because. Randy's happy right now. And we always do everything together."

DONALD WAS HERE

8:01 P.M., Panama City, Florida—Donald Trump is in town. My wife and I are in a nearby barbecue joint. There are so many cars in this city, my pork tastes like exhaust.

Twenty-one thousand folks of every shape and size are here. Old ladies in red caps, dogs in flag-sweaters, elderly men with patriotic koozies. Cops, teachers, Girl Scouts.

The woman in the booth next to us asks, "Y'all going to the rally?"

"No ma'am," I say. "We prefer NASCAR to dirt tracks."

The truth is, you won't meet anyone less political than me. I did not grow up playing the sport.

The most political event I've attended was a livestock auction. Bill Branner was running for reelection. He passed out paper fans with the words: "Be a fan for Brann'" printed on them.

That night, every cow pie in three counties had fans poking from the tops.

Look, I don't have anything against politicians—red, blue, or polka-dot. My problem is with the human race. People are selfish and mean. And I'm not talking about candidates. I'm talking about us.

Consider Tyler, whose mother just died, whose father just went to jail for child pornography. Where's Tyler going to spend Christmas? Doesn't anyone care about him?

What about Anne? Her daughter got raped, killed, and stuffed in a trunk. Or: Rena—going through chemo, ashamed of how puffy and bald she looks. These are the ones I'm interested in.

Life is no picnic. We have terrorists, cyber-wars, mutating bacteria, and deadly mosquitoes. And if they don't get you, teenagers who dress up like killer clowns from Hell will.

As it happens, my grandaddy often told a story about Hell.

"Hell ain't what you think," he'd say. "Ain't no flames, dragons, or pitchforks. Hell is one big feast—with biscuits, ribs, creamed corn, butter beans, cheese grits, pulled pork..."

Bear with me here.

"Thing is," he'd go on. "People in Hell can't eat because their arms don't bend. No matter how they try, they can't get food to their mouths."

Well, I have experience in this department. I once broke my arm at ball practice and had to wear a cast. Try eating drumsticks with your humerus in cement. I lost two pant-sizes.

"Up Yonder," Grandaddy would say. "They have the same problems as in Hell. Same table with food, same stiff arms."

"But," I'd point out. "If that's how Heaven is, why would anyone ever want to go there?"

"'Cause," he'd say. "People in Heaven feed each other."

Well.

What I mean to say is: I don't give a damn who you vote for. But if you really want to change the world...

Go love somebody.

BOUND FOR ALABAMA

She's been living in the South four years, but can't seem to get Chicago out of her accent. She waits tables in Mobile. All her customers notice the way she talks. Her regulars kid her about it.

"I try saying, '*y'all*' sometimes," she said. "But it never comes out right."

It's okay. Truth told, I hear more Southern teenagers using Yankee birdcalls such as: "you guys." They say it with a drawl. It comes out sounding like, "You *gahz.*"

I blame the Internet.

"I've always wanted to live in the South," she said. "Always felt I should'a been born here. Something about it."

She's no spring chick. She has lines around her eyes, a wiry frame, and her hands look strong. I asked how she came to the area.

"Moved here after my husband tried to kill me."

I could tell she wasn't being funny. So, I quit asking questions and made a remark about the weather.

She kept on, "Since he couldn't kill me, my husband ended up killing himself, and our son. Ran the car right off the road, hit a tree. Looked like an accident, but I know it wasn't."

Jesus.

"I went from being a wife and a mother to being nothing. It was hard."

After they passed, she quit taking care of herself. Her days consisted of Hamburger Helper, Marlboro Reds, and long bouts of crying.

A friend suggested she see a therapist. So, she looked one up in the phonebook.

"Didn't even know what I was looking for," she said. "Just stuck my finger on a name and made an appointment."

And as fate would have it—if you believe in that sort of thing—the therapist was a widow who'd lost her child, too.

"When my therapist opened her mouth," she went on. "She had a Southern accent, sounded so warm and friendly... I just really bonded with her."

The Georgia-born therapist suggested traveling. But life decisions are easier talked about than made. So fate helped her out again.

Her boss fired her.

"That was the last straw," she said. "I was like, 'You know, I'm gonna go visit the Southeast. What do I have to lose?'"

Nothing.

So, for the first time she pointed her tires south. Four weeks she traveled. She treated herself to hotels, restaurants, and even walked some of the Appalachian Trail. And when she hit Gulf Shores, she decided once and for all: no more Chicago.

"I feel like my life is starting, even at my age. I know I'm not a Southerner, but I really like it here."

Darling, you're more than Southern.

You're home.

WAR EAGLE WOMAN

For a funeral, it was a nice one. They say she looked good. She represented Auburn to the end, wearing orange and blue—and eagle broach. I understand her artificial smile set off her outfit.

Her kids weren't enthusiastic about her get-up, but before she died she'd made her wishes were clear.

"The funny thing," her son says. "She didn't go to Auburn. None of us did. Actually, I don't even know if my mother finished high school."

Truth told, her kids don't know much about her early days. What they do know, they cherish. Now that she's gone, they wish they'd asked more questions.

Hindsight.

She was the eldest of five. Her mother died young. After her mother passed, she raised her siblings. She changed diapers, prepared suppers, and they say her father was too familiar with her.

"When she married my dad," he says. "She was twenty-five. She'd already reared a family at that age. My uncles and aunts all treated her like their mother."

She had a good adult life. She bore three kids, made sack lunches, and knew her way around an oven roast. To her children she's a saint.

"My mother never got mad," he says. "Like when I

got arrested for driving drunk. Mother came to pick me up. She never even addressed it. I'm sure she was was upset, but she just told me, 'Son, I forgive you.'"

She forgave him so intensively, she made him paint their entire two-story home using a paintbrush and Campbell's soup can.

"She adored my dad," he adds. "He was like her second shot at a normal life. To make up for her childhood, Dad was so good to her. He let her be herself."

And thats how she came to show interest in Auburn football. The couple worshiped the SEC calendar. She started pulling for the Tigers to tease her husband—a committed Alabama fan. On the weekends, she'd aggravate the stew out of him by wearing Auburn colors.

He'd pick on her.

When he developed dementia, the games became important rituals. She'd visit his assisted living facility on weekends for gameday. And as long as she wore her colors, he recognized her.

"The day of her funeral," he goes on. "We all wore orange and blue. Dad even wore a bright orange jacket and blue tie. I'd never seen him wear those colors before.

"We all felt kinda ridiculous. But when she told us what colors she wanted to be buried in... I dunno, if she could'a seen us, reckon we would'a made her proud."

Yes.

I reckon you would have.

IN THE WOODS

The doctors gave him a few years, tops. He says he's not afraid.

He spends a lot of time in the woods. He's been this way since childhood. Chances are, if you don't find him in the forest, you probably won't find him.

A few weeks ago, I visited. We went for a walk near his house.

He looks good. He's bald. His hair is growing back in patches. He covers it with an Ole' Miss cap. Once upon a time, I would've given him hell about Alabama's recent victory against the Rebels. Not now.

They first discovered his cancer when he was young. They operated; he thought he was cured. For a long time, he seemed all right. Then he started going downhill. He's forty-three now—and a ways down the hill.

"My body hates me," he said. "I've come to terms with that. But I'm not my body. I just live in it, lotta people don't get that."

Well, to tell you the truth, I don't get it, either. But then, I never claimed to be smart.

"I ain't worried about dying," he went on. "I mean, it's sad, but this life ain't all there is."

Well, I've thumbed through afterlife theories before. I've had a hard time making heads or tails. I've heard enough to confuse me.

A college professor once told me there was no hereafter—he emphasized that everything either becomes worm poop or limestone. My mother believes in streets of gold. My deranged uncle believes we come back as possums. My wife believes her father is a turkey buzzard.

"Oh, I believe there's a Heaven," he said. "I have to."

We stopped to look at the pine trees. He still loves them. When he was younger and more agile, he could scale them like a monkey. Now, he just looks upward.

"God gave me a gift," he said. "Letting me get this sick."

Yeah? Well, I don't see it that way. Life has dished him some hateful blows without having the decency to give him a reason.

"No, I mean it," he said. "I'm really lucky. Been thinking about death for so many years, I'm not even scared of it anymore. You learn a lot when you get over the fear of dying. People go their whole lives without knowing what it's all about."

I hated to ask the idiotic question of the century, but I asked what it was all about.

He ignored my question, too deep in thought, I guess.

"Hey," he finally said. "When you write your story thing, will you say in there that I love my wife and kids? Maybe they'll read it when I'm gone, and remember that love."

I'll aim for more than that.

I'm going to tell every person I know.

HE HATES THE SOUTH

"I hate the South," he shouts to the bar. "I miss living in Philly."

He's an obnoxious fella, ten-times my size, drunk as Cooter Brown.

"Rednecks," he goes on, ordering a whiskey sour. "Everyone's racist, they don't know jack $#!+ about the world, prolly can't even SPELL Philadelphia."

This is an affront.

Willa, the bartender, accepts his challenge. She concentrates, then scribbles the word on a napkin.

He cackles. "Oh my GOD! There's no F in Philadelphia!"

He celebrates with another whiskey.

Willa's embarrassed. She's from Oxford—a city once named Lick Skillet before the Union Army came along.

"You ignorant girl," he says. "Didn't you even go to SCHOOL?"

Now wait just a hot minute.

Look, say what you want about the South. Heckle all day. But when you insult a woman's intelligence, it's time to have a little talk with Jesus.

The idea that those below the Mason Dixon are racist bumpkins—ridden with poor dental genetics—lacking enough smarts to spell Poughkeepsie, is loathsome.

First off: I just spelled it.

Second: spell Czechoslovakia.

We aren't Philadelphians. We don't eat much cream cheese. And we don't drink whiskey sours—putting eggs in your bourbon would get you shot in some parts.

But we're not so different. We're humans, same as Yankees, Canadians, East Europeans, and good spellers. Sure, we have gross racists. So does Boston.

We also have exceptional people.

Such as, Caroline—a white-haired woman with fourteen black boys living in her house. They're college baseball players. In exchange for room and meals, they maintain her antique home. They're well-behaved, straight-A students.

Daryl—from a town no bigger than a postage stamp. His teachers noticed how smart he was when he practiced math on the sidewalk in chalk. Today, he works for the Pentagon.

Michelle—a six-foot-five, black, lesbian who found a toddler underneath a bridge, then adopted him. I dare you to stereotype her.

Don—a Georgia man who gave a minivan to a homeless woman.

Or: the Louisiana girl missing her leg, who competed in a triathlon.

What about the Methodist chaplain who sat with an eighty-three-year-old Muslim at his deathbed? Both had the gall to call each other brothers.

This is Dixie, not Idiotville, pal.

Here, men know how to field dress squirrels, women glide when they walk. Lilies grow in ditches, kudzu grows on kudzu. The Bible gets quoted by old ladies, drug addicts, and everyone in between. Hospitality is free. Tea is sweet enough to give you kidney stones.

Maybe you are miserable here. And, well, I'm sorry to hear that.

Some of us wouldn't trade it for all the cream cheese in Filadelfia.

THE TURKEY HILL HEALER

Maw Maw is ninety-seven today, and sharp as a jack knife. Well, she might be really ninety-eight. Her granddaughter says her birth certificate and Social Security Card don't match.

Anyway, government paper wasn't vital in 1918. Not compared to things like prayer, food, the Bible, or enduring flu pandemics.

Things have changed.

"She grew up in Turkey Hill," her granddaughter says. "Everyone knows her by her real name, Ozenia. She hates being inside, loves outdoor things like blackberry picking, or gardening..."

Her granddaughter shows me a photograph that goes way back.

The woman is a leftover from Alabamian history. She has Native American blood. High cheeks, blue-black hair, a glare hard as the flat-side of a skillet.

And old time religion.

The ancient kind without air conditioning, stadium seating, or headset microphones. The rural sort, with faith healers who could raise the dead.

She was reared in the days when radio was witchcraft. When girls went shoeless, and boys called them, ma'am, or Mama. When children knew how to fend off cottonmouths with nothing but faith and garden hoes.

"When we were kids," her granddaughter goes on. "She carried a hickory switch in her purse. She didn't spare the rod... That woman fears the Lord."

She does more than fear him, she speaks in tongues to him. She'll tell you about healings and miracles she's seen over the years. And she can even help you get one.

Maw Maw is part of a generation who sees prayer and weeping as going hand in hand. Who believes God can make something out of nothing. She may be old, but her heart isn't.

"After church," her granddaughter says. "She always visited the nursing homes. She'd bake cakes, take'em with her. She'd ask if we wanted to go. We rarely did."

Today, Maw Maw lives on her own, does her own laundry, doles her meds, has her teeth, and will be doggone if anyone cooks for her.

Truth told, life isn't much different for Ozenia than it has been. She still wakes early. She still drinks Sanka—black as soot—then reads her Bible and bows her head to move a mountain or two.

When asked about her birthday, Maw Maw says with a smile, "My time here is short."

I suppose she's right. Life for anyone is a flicker. Even for Baptists and Pentecostals. Just when you think you've got the hang of it, you realize your oven timer's about to go off. But to her this is no curse, it's a privilege.

Because some glad morning when this life is over, Maw Maw plans on going into the miracle business full-time.

Until then, happy ninety-seventh birthday, Ozenia.

Or ninety-eighth.

GOOD HUNTING

He had leukemia. If he'd been older, he might've been bitter about it. But he wasn't. Nine-year-olds don't know how to feel such things.

He spent his days in a camouflage recliner, staring at a laptop. He didn't have much energy for anything more than browsing the Internet. What he did have, however, was friends all over the Southeast. People he'd met on online hunting sites.

"They were older than he was," his mother said. "But they meant a lot to him. He was always talking this'n that about them."

She means fellas like—we'll call him, Rob—a fifty-six-year-old deer hunter from middle Tennessee.

Rob said, "Didn't know he was so young when we first messaged. We became big buddies. He'd never been hunting and liked reading about it. I like to talk hunting, so it worked..."

He confided in Rob. He told him about his illness. About his daddy, who once promised to take him hunting, but died before he ever got the chance.

"Every time we wrote," Rob said. "I'd think of my own boy, and how fast life can change. Sometimes my wife'd find me crying at the computer."

One day, Rob woke to see a post to the group, asking

if anyone in his area might take him hunting on the weekend before he underwent invasive treatment.

"I felt something in me," said Rob. "I just thought, you know, this kid ain't got nothing, all he wants to do is kill a spike. Nobody was replying. Broke my heart."

So Rob called the boy's mother and made plans. He took off work, drove to Alabama for the weekend. His friends thought it was bizarre.

And on the Saturday Rob arrived at his house, he found other trucks parked in the driveway. Each with Browning, Winchester, and Remington stickers on the tailgates.

"They were other guys from the group," said Rob. "One came all the way from frickin' Missouri."

They met him.

"We expected some weak-looking kid. But he didn't look bad, except he was bald."

Thus, that Saturday, six men, four boys, and one leukemia patient went hunting. The kid killed a buck. And according to Rob: "I never seen a boy happier. It was a good hunt, a blessing."

The young fella gave up the fight. On his casket his mother says there was a photograph. The boy smiling, grasping antlers. Several men stand around him wearing orange caps.

"I hope God's got plenty'a whitetails up there," said Rob. "He knows what he's doing now."

Yes.

I believe he does.

THE DAMNED EVENING NEWS

Montgomery, Alabama—the meat department. I stood behind them. They were Mexican. Maybe fourteen. Faded caps. Ratty jeans. Clothes covered in dirt and mortar. Skinny as a flock of number-two pencils.

They ordered a half-pound of beef.

The butcher handed them enough wrapped packages to sink the U.S.S. Alabama.

One kid remarked, "What this? We only ask for half pound."

The butcher said, "Aw, it's free. I have to get rid of it. Expiration date's today. Freeze it, it'll last for years."

The boys looked like they'd just discovered teeth.

One said, "God bless joo, sir."

Pensacola, Florida—Cracker Barrel parking lot. I saw a man with his wife. Maybe it was his girlfriend. She was in a wheelchair. She had blonde hair. She couldn't stop twitching.

He rolled her into the restaurant. She dropped her purse. He picked it up.

She moaned, "I'm so sorry, honey."

He kissed her. "Don't ever apologize to me, silly."

Silly.

Macon, Georgia— Walmart. A man and his kids

stood in the checkout lane. They had a basket with a few things. He swiped his card. It wouldn't go.

The cashier said, "Sorry sir, this card's denied."

His face changed. He turned to leave.

The lady behind him stepped forward, removed her wallet, and said, "How much?" She paid for his groceries.

He thanked her.

She answered matter-of-factly, "I'm a single mother, I know what it's like being broke."

How about this one:

Defuniak Springs, Florida—I saw an elderly man with car trouble at the gas station. The clerk—in her mid-twenties—rushed outside to help. She got his car started. The man tipped her ten bucks.

The clerk took the money and said, "You have NO idea how bad I needed this today."

So he dug into his pocket and gave her more bills. Handfuls.

Listen, while I write this the news is playing on television. The announcer reads headlines. Shootings, stabbings, rapes, racism, pressure-cooker bombs. He's using a polished, monotone voice.

Then: more footage from the recent presidential debates, various missile launches, a Brad Pitt divorce, mushroom clouds. And in case you fell asleep, candidate polls.

I'm a nobody from nowhere. Admittedly, I drink warm beer, and I have nary a credential to my hillbilly name. I have no right to tell anyone how to do their job. Truth told, I have a hard enough time just emptying the dishwasher.

But if I may, I'd like to say something to the broadcast journalists who dredge up shocking headlines every day.

Brothers and sisters...

You're looking in all the wrong damn places.
Try the meat department.

FUNERAL FOOD

My father died on a Wednesday. On Thursday morning, my aunt was already in the kitchen cooking.

Pound cakes, fried chicken, smothered dove, enough gravy to be a felony.

My aunt also covered our mirrors with blankets. I asked why she did such a thing.

She said, "Same reason I'm cooking, it's what we do."

Well, nobody tells you death and food go hand in hand. When someone dies, an explosion of casseroles follow. Our front porch nearly buckled from the weight of the covered dishes.

We received food of all kinds. The man down the road delivered bullfrog legs. One lady brought tomatoes in jars. Someone even brought a garbage bag of green peanuts.

I wish I could tell you how it all tasted. But I can't. After daddy's funeral, everything was bland.

Anyway, my wife cooks for funerals, too. I've seen her whip up enough to fill two city blocks.

A few years ago, a man died. She broke her back making more food than I've ever seen. She slaved for days in the kitchen—popping Advil. When all was finished, our galley looked like a grease pit.

That night, we loaded coolers into my truck. She sat

in the passenger seat, balancing casseroles on her lap. When we made the drop, a boy met us at the door, which took me off guard. I didn't know the man had kids.

The boy eyed the dishes.

I forced a smile past the lump in my throat.

His hair was redder than mine.

Later, he and I sat on the porch. He didn't have much to say. When he eventually did speak, he said, "Why'd you bring so much food?"

I couldn't answer.

The truth is, I'm not sure why. God knows, he wasn't going to enjoy it no matter how much he ate. And that's a shame—my wife makes exceptional biscuits.

But, I've thought about it a lot since that day. And If I'd been in my right mind, I might've told him:

Son, one day years from now, that ache in your chest will still be there. I'm sorry to be the one to tell you that. But you'll get used to it.

And when you see someone else suffer, it will only get worse. But this isn't a bad hurt. Because it'll make you remember.

Immediately, you'll get reminded of all this food. Maybe you'll have warm memories of your aunt—and how superstitious she was. Remember how alone you felt.

Maybe you'll remember all the covered dishes, and how some folks didn't know what to say, so they kept quiet. Some sat with you, watching the night sky. Several prayed for you. Some still do.

Then you'll realize something and it will all become clear to you.

It wasn't food those people gave.

It was love.

ALABAMA SINGLE-WIDE

Her husband left her with two boys. And since money didn't grow in the backyard, she worked more than one thankless job.

One morning, she found a stray dog on her porch, stealing food from her cats. She tore out the door and shouted. A man came out of the woods to fetch the dog. He was bearded. Dirty. Homeless. He apologized profusely.

The next morning, she found a brand new bag of food on her porch.

She got to know the man, introduced him to her boys. The next thing she knew, she'd put him up in her guest bedroom. She took him to a barber, helped him get a job, even let him use her car. After a few months, he found an apartment.

One that allowed pets.

"Couldn't believe how fast it happened," she said. "I realized, 'Hey, you ain't gotta be rich to make a difference in someone's life.'"

That's when she started volunteering at the local rescue mission with her boys. They started serving meals, washing dishes, rocking babies to sleep. Soon, she volunteered more often than she worked her regular job.

"Was a real eye-opener," she went on. "So many addicts, crazy folks out there, and kids, too."

Kids.

One of the children she's talking about was a toddler who I'll call Briana—whose mother was dying from drug-related problems. The two shared an instant connection.

"I just knew I had to do something for that girl."

So, she approached Briana's dying mother with a proposition.

"I asked about adopting her. I was afraid I's gonna offend her, but she just said, 'I've been praying you'd ask me that.'"

She paused to wipe an eye. "She died a few weeks later."

Briana got her own room—decorated in green, which is her favorite color. Her closet was loaded with new clothes and shoes. Her bed had Disney sheets. As it happened, Briana had only ever slept on cots before. It was her first mattress.

"She didn't even sleep in it. The first night, she was so scared she slept with me. We did that for a long time until she finally felt okay in her own room."

But that was a long time ago. Briana's grown up now. Today, she's married. She calls her adopted mother twice —sometimes three times—per day. They're best friends.

"I'm so proud of her," she said of her daughter. "I just hope and pray I was a good mother. I mean, I raised all my kids in an old single-wide, we had hard times, we did without. I ain't exactly mother of the year."

Respectfully, ma'am.

The hell you ain't.

TOUGH GIRLS

Rural Florida. The Depression was alive and kicking.

This was a time when folks sat on porches, swatting gnats. Fathers gave out bottle-caps for allowances, mothers canned anything with seeds. Ketchup was six cents a bottle.

She was a striking seventeen-year-old with honey-blonde hair—like her mother. She was dating the son of a wealthy man—an arrogant, rowdy kid.

One night, the boy got half tight and broke into the girl's house. Only, she was out that night. He forced himself on her young widowed mother. He violated her. He broke her collar bone.

Her mother didn't tell anyone.

It wasn't long afterward, her mother started noticing morning nausea, and her clothes got tight.

Her mother decided to end the pregnancy. After working up the courage, she drove to visit the amateur doctor on the edge of town—a man who fixed things.

She sat on a wood table with her skirt off, crying too hard to go through with it. She left. And she hated herself for even considering it.

Months went by, she developed a tummy. People in town punished her with words like, "hussy," and, "whore."

And on the day her daughter found her sobbing on the kitchen floor, she extracted the truth from her.

They left town for a fresh start, rented a city apartment. Menial jobs paid the bills. Sometimes, chicken soup looked like saltwater—provided they were lucky enough to have salt.

Those were merciless days, and they got worse.

Her mother had complications during labor. She bled to death. And because she was destitute, the county classified her as a, "necessary burial."

She got a pinewood box. No marker.

With her mother gone, she claimed her newborn brother as her son. She met a man while working in a cotton factory. And with the help of her new husband, she raised the boy everyone believed was hers.

When the economy improved, so did lives.

The boy had an ordinary childhood. Two parents; three-bedroom house. He played jacks, hop-scotch, and learned to shoot bee-bee guns. He became a man. He went to a decent university, made a life, took a wife.

A lifetime later, her honey hair turned white. She fought illness. Before it killed her, the boy she raised sat beside her.

In between crying fits, he asked, "Why is life so unfair, mama?"

She smiled. "Unfair? I didn't raise you to complain that'a way. Life's a blessing."

A blessing.

He disagreed.

So, she told him everything I just told you.

JAMIE

When I asked her to marry me, I gave her the world's tiniest diamond.

I bought the ring with cash I'd hoarded in an Altoids tin. I walked into the jeweler and said, "Give me whatever this'll buy."

He said, "This is the smallest diamond we got, sir."

I left with a small box and a promise to pay the twenty-seven-dollars I still owed.

She wore a red blouse the night I fumbled my proposal. It surprised me when she said yes. She could've married a man of means—or at least someone with a nicer truck.

Instead, she got a rock the size of an Oxford comma.

To celebrate, we ate at one of those meat-and-three places. We ran into my uncle. Jamie showed him the ring.

He squinted and said, "Lord, if that thing were any smaller it'd belong in a saltshaker."

Uncles.

Our wedding was in December, our honeymoon landed on Christmas. I wanted to get her a gift, so I bought a carriage ride and a carton of ice cream.

We moved into an apartment the size of a turnip crate. We ate Hamburger Helper for suppers. We had no internet, cellphones, or cable. Instead, we played poker on the floor using Cheez-Its.

She taught preschool. I crawled on people's roofs with a hammer. In the evenings, we'd eat supper and say painfully corny things like: "I can't believe we're really married, can you?"

"Don't it beat all?" the other would say. "You want some ice cream?"

You bet your Barbie Ring I do.

Then, we'd sit in the den eating, watching a console television I'd salvaged from a roadside garbage pile. When the picture got fuzzy, Jamie would cuss and kick until it improved—making her popular with the downstairs neighbors.

The fact is, our lives have been average. We've buried good dogs together, totaled two trucks, and lost one mobile home.

Last spring, they found a lump in her. They took her in for tests. A nurse led us into a sterile room and asked her to remove all jewelry. I tried to be tough.

I failed.

Jamie took off her ring. I'd forgotten how small the thing was. All I could think about were red blouses, carriage rides, and console televisions.

"Please take good care of that," she said, laying it in my palm. "It's the most valuable thing I've ever had."

And when they took her away, wearing her god-awful gown, sitting in that god-forsaken wheelchair, I said the same thing to God.

And even though the Big Man doesn't owe me nary a thing in this life, sometimes I look at that puny ring...

And remember He's held up his end of the bargain.

DUST TO DUST

Sometimes when they cremate people they put them in cardboard boxes. At the crematory, we signed a release form and got a hundred-pound box in return.

This suited Daddy fine. He thought fancy urns were ridiculous.

"When I die," he said once. "Don't keep me around, collecting dust. Turn me loose, let me be with the Lord."

After he died, he was anything but loose. He came tightly packed in what looked like Priority Mail. We kept him in the laundry room for a few months. I sat beside him carrying on one-sided conversations.

He didn't have much to say.

He passed during the worst possible time of year. It was mid-football season. I listened to games on a pocket radio, sitting beside his cardboard mortuary.

"Touchdown," I'd say.

He'd agree.

Eventually, we scattered Daddy in the mountains. Only he didn't scatter. His remains were too compressed. They stuck together like a gray brick.

There were no dramatic wind gusts. No orchestras. He fell seven-hundred feet like old mud, then crumbled.

And that's how it happened. I was supposed to set him free, but I didn't. His ashes might've been loose, but

I kept him around for years. I brought him along for fishing trips, dates, weddings, barbecues, and baseball games.

Because there were few things worse than watching baseball alone.

Anyway, last week my wife and I walked the beach. I saw a man and his family having a funeral near the surf. He held what looked like an elaborate coffee pot. People stood in a semi-circle.

Strangers along the shore quit walking when they got close. Folks folded hands and bowed heads. We did the same thing. There must've been ten of us.

The man flung the dust into the waves. The wind caught it and whipped it into a big pattern in the air. It was poetry.

Some folks get all the luck.

The man embraced a woman—his wife, maybe. They cried. Most people kept their heads down. My allergies started acting up. My wife asked if I was okay.

"Pollen's bad this time of year," said I.

The thing is, it's been a long time since Daddy left. I'm an adult now. I have arthritis in my feet, a mortgage, a pair of reading glasses, and I can't eat pizza past five.

But one thing's remained the same. I've kept a tight grip on him. The good, the bad, and the repulsive. I guess what I'm trying to say is:

Daddy, you're missing a good World Series this year. But I don't mind watching it alone.

I'm ready now.

Go be with the Lord.

TEACHERS AMONG US

He wasn't a bad kid. He just acted out in class. His teacher knew something was wrong at home, but she didn't know what to do. So she went easy on him.

Rookie mistake.

"Nicer I was," she said. "The more he acted out. He wanted attention."

So she gave him the positive kind. She moved his desk, praised him for hard work. She even gave him rides home.

When she dropped him off, she noticed his mother wasn't around.

"Where's you're mother?" she once asked.

"She's getting clean-o-therapy," he said. "It makes her cancer better."

That's when her heart broke. She did what any God-fearing woman would. She rushed home and cooked up a whirlwind. Cookies, cakes, cornbread, and casseroles.

She stopped by the following day. His mother was napping. So, she snooped around his house. The place was a hog pen. No toilet paper, no snacks, and the refrigerator was a wasteland.

"When I met his mother," she went on. "She was in a bad way. Her hair was gone. No wonder she didn't have food, she could hardly talk."

The teacher asked her Bible study group for help. They raised money, bought groceries. A handful of ladies cooked suppers. Some donated money.

His mother died suddenly.

The family couldn't afford a funeral. His grades dropped. His uncle moved in. He started skipping school.

"I had to do something," she said. "Or else I knew he'd be another statistic."

She began spending time with him. She carried him to waterparks, movies, malls, church parties, you name it. She celebrated his birthdays, Thanksgivings, Christmases, and all other occasions. He even lived with her for six weeks when his uncle was out of town.

She wedged herself into the kid's life and didn't let go.

Then he moved away. They lost touch.

A few dozen years have passed by. She doesn't look like the young photograph she showed me. Her hair is grayer. She's raised two college-age girls, married twice.

She still teaches.

A few months ago, a visitor stopped by her classroom unannounced. A six-foot-eight giant who'd just gotten out of the Army.

She knew that face.

He hugged her neck and said, "I just wanna thank you, Mrs. Audrey. You're the reason for everything good in my world."

"You know," she said. "Maybe I've only touched one life, but as a teacher, one's enough."

Maybe so. But you ought to know something: you've touched more than one.

You've certainly touched me.

And today, I have a feeling you're going to touch a few more.

GOD IS HATE

He wore a sign on his chest that read: "God hates fags." He paced the sidewalk, waving a Bible like it was a firearm.

The street-preacher zeroed in on me. He fired several ugly words in my direction. And true to his sandwich-sign, he was downright hateful.

I told him God didn't hate anybody.

He told me to go to Hell.

From the looks of it, he was leading the way.

The first thing you should know is that I was raised in church. My people are the rural kind who believe in covered dishes, homecomings, and canned-food drives at Christmas.

The truth is, I don't talk religion. I remember the words of Grandaddy, who said: "Don't talk politics or religion in mixed company—and always carry toilet paper in your glovebox."

Sound advice.

Even so, I cannot abide rudeness. My people have come too far to be represented by Eddie the Evangelical in a plywood jumpsuit.

Besides, he's got it all wrong. And it's not fair to let him tinkle in our tea.

It's not fair to Anne Miller—a seventy-year-old

widow who adopted a teenage prostitute, then raised her crack-addicted baby.

It dishonors the legacy of Terry Johnson—with his weekly barbecues for fatherless boys. Who taught hundreds how to throw footballs, crank fishing reels, and swing Louisville Sluggers.

I don't care what the hand-painted sign says. This kid's never met Sister Caroline—a lesbian nun who started a women's halfway house in an auto garage.

Or: Penny Dugan—mother of three. Whose husband said he'd been cheating on her with a man. He explained he was HIV positive. Penny nursed him until his death, then she cared for his dying boyfriend—and thousands more AIDS victims thereafter.

Thousands.

Dammit, this isn't religion. This is my heritage you're lifting your leg on. And as a card-carrying member of the Little Brown Church in the Vale, I'm obliged to tell you:

God isn't hate.

He's not that kind of fella. He cares for preachers the same as he does serial killers, fisherman, bloodhounds, and Barney Fife.

He even loves rapists; the man who murdered his wife and kids; the man who robbed the Tom Thumb; the alcoholic bleeding to death on the kitchen floor; the kid I met in Birmingham who lives under a bridge. He loves divorcees, baseball fanatics, orphans, those who mourn, veterans, non-voters, LSU fans, and the big-nosed dummy writing this.

Now take off that sign before you get a splinter in you hindparts. God loves you, kid. And even though you're breaking His heart...

So do I.

WHAT I HOPE

I hope you find money today. It doesn't have to be much. Just a little. Few things are better than finding an unexpected twenty in a coat pocket. It's the universe's way of saying, "It's gonna work out, pal."

And I believe this.

Of course, I don't know how it will work out. But I believe it will. And I believe it's going to happen sooner than you think.

When you find your cash, remember that.

I had a friend who could find money wherever he went. It was an unusual talent. He could spot quarters, nickels, dimes, and pennies in any parking lot, sidewalk, or covered garage. I wish I could do that.

Believe me, I've tried.

Once, he found a fifty while walking into a theater. Another time: a hundred-dollar bill in a sewer. Another time: he found a woman's wallet stuffed with three thousand bucks.

He took the wallet to the sheriff's. After a few days, a woman claimed it. The deputies said the owner was a widow with three kids. To show her thanks, she left a hundred dollars at the police station as a finder's prize.

My friend didn't want a reward. He used the cash, and a few hundred dollars more, to buy a Pizza Hut gift card. He hand delivered it to the woman.

"Why would you do that?" I asked.

"Because, I'm a single dad," he said. "Cooking for kids every single night is Purgatory. Every kid likes pizza."

Anyway, maybe you cook every night. And maybe you're not sure anyone realizes how hard you work. You've been running hot for so long, with such little recognition, sometimes you feel like wet toilet paper on a public restroom floor.

Feeling invisible can be the same as dying.

Or: you might feel alone. God forbid. I can't think of anything worse than loneliness. It sucks the energy out of a man. I wouldn't wish this feeling on my worst enemy.

Perhaps your confidence has dried up. At one time, you felt like you had the world by the steering wheel. Now you feel about as special as a bowlful of Shredded Wheat.

I'm sorry. God help me, I am.

Look, I'm no expert. I can't give you a lick of advice about life because I'm nothing. I'm Joe Six-Pack who's writing because he can't sleep right now. I'm not qualified to train a skunk to stink.

But if you're reading this, I'm talking to you. I'm pulling for you. I'm hoping you get your miracle. I'm hoping you feel loved.

But above all.

I hope you find some money.

FISHERBOY

He was two-foot tall, happy faced, chubby. He had the gift of gab. He stood at the public boat ramp eating Cheetos, holding a cheap rod and reel.

The little fella's first words to me were: "I guess fish hate me."

Welcome to the club, Tex.

We talked about things. About life. The weather. It doesn't take long to make fast friends with chubby, chatty kids.

I should know, I was one.

That weekend, his mother bought him a fishing rod, wrapped it in a red ribbon, and left him a note reading: "No more video games. Go fishing today. Love, Mom."

He rode his bike to the public boat launch and that's where he met me.

The truth is, there were better teachers. I'm a mediocre fisherman at best. Even so, I did my utmost to show him how to tie knots, how to cast, and how to yank a popping cork hard enough to frighten millions of innocent sea creatures.

He was clumsy. The same as I was during childhood. It took some practice, but underneath all his baby fat was a natural.

He caught a trout. It was his first one. Tiny.

He shouted, "This is the greatest day of my LIFE!!"

And he meant it.

We drank gas-station Coca-Cola and ate potato chips. He did all the talking.

He carried on about fighter jets, rifles, and his runaway father—who left earlier that year. Who never picked up the phone thereafter.

I told him I was sorry.

He shrugged, saying, "Aw, it's okay, I don't even care about my old man."

Liar.

Before he bid me goodbye he reminded me it was indeed the greatest day of his existence.

That was a lifetime ago.

Yesterday, I wouldn't have recognized him. He's a grown-up. He had a toddler with him. She was fidgety. She tried to say my name, but the task proved insurmountable.

He pumped my hand and said, "God, you look old!"

I thanked him for his unsolicited compliment.

He's an electrician. He's got three kids. A house. A life. It made me proud.

"I've thought about you," he added. "Do you remember that day I caught that fish?"

Do I.

I haven't done much in life, son. But even if I had, I'd never forget that Saturday.

It's not every day you meet a kid who has so much to say, he runs out of breath mid-sentence. Who reminds you of yourself. Who just wants to feel like somebody's son once in a while.

It's not often you see the greatest day of someone's life.

IN MEMORY OF TOM

He drank too much. I knew that about him. Other than that, I didn't know much more than his first name.

Which was Tom.

He had long hair, a yellowed beard. He was wiry. He smelled like the backend of a poultry truck. His breath could knock over a two-bedroom house.

Occasionally, his breath smelled minty.

Tom told me once, with a hoarse laugh. "I sip mouthwash sometimes. In a pinch, it'll give you a good buzz, but it burns like hell."

I'll bet.

He frequented a restaurant I worked at, looking for handouts. He only visited when certain employees were on shift.

He knew which workers gave out free food or money, and which ones told him to get lost.

He carried a duffel bag. Olive green. He wore the same camouflage shirt. He didn't know a stranger.

And nobody knew his full name.

I visited that restaurant a few weeks ago. It's been a long time. I asked the waiter if they ever had any homeless loiter nearby.

He called the manager over.

"You mean Tom?" the manager said. "He used'a

come around a lot. But, well, he..."

I had a feeling.

He went on, "One day Tom walked in and said he couldn't get a deep breath. I wasn't working that day."

An employee took Tom to the emergency room. He had pneumonia. Bad. They hospitalized him. The infection killed him. The county got his body. What happened to his remains, nobody could say.

I never thought I'd write about him. Truthfully, I don't think he would've cared for it.

But this is the South, and we have a longstanding tradition. We write obituaries for our departed, honoring them in print. A few sentences is the privilege of every man—be he rich, poor, or vagrant drunk.

Tom deserves his.

And so:

"Tom was heralded into Glory March 2015. Nobody remembers his full name, or where he came from. But as a young man he fought in Vietnam. And he was proud of that.

"He was meek, poor in spirit, and a member of the human race. He died without making a sound. But he'll be remembered for his cheerfulness and God-given sense of humor—even in the face of poverty.

"As far as anyone knows, he left no family, no possessions, and had no memorial services. Because the truth is, he went unnoticed by the rest of the world.

"But today, he has no afflictions, no sadness, and no bottle. And you can find him spending time with the One who kept him fed for so many years. His friend.

"The One who knows Tom's full name."

Rest well, Tom.

Rest.

EXTRA INNING

I watched the World Series with a ghost. He sat beside me cussing at the television. He threw his hands up. He degraded umpires.

And when the game went into rain-delay, he told me to get him a beer.

"But, you're a ghost," said I.

"Then you'll have to drink it for me," he said.

If he would've lived long enough, he might've been one of those old timers who told the same stories over and over.

"I ever tell you," he'd begin, "the time I pitched sixteen innings against the Catholic team?"

Only a hundred and seventy times.

He'd go on, "There were nuns in the stands..."

I know. They trash-talked worse than sailors, and called you sugar-britches.

"Them nuns talked trash worse'n a bunch of sailors, they called me..."

Daddy auditioned for a double-A ball club, long ago. He made it. But he only lasted a hot minute. They cut him. His dreams were dashed. He said it was the best gift God ever gave him.

"Cocky folks don't get nowhere in life," he said. "I was young. I needed to be humbled, never played another *real* game after that."

And as far as I know, he didn't.

Even so, he coached Little League. He'd chew Juicy Fruit in a dugout and praise fifteen uncoordinated, moderately pathetic boys.

He'd shout things like, "Good hustle!"

The highest praise a chubby boy can get.

We played catch nearly every night during summer. He threw light and easy.

When the sun would lower, he'd say, "We'd better go inside or we'll be eating fastballs."

I didn't think he could throw fastballs.

But before he died I saw him pitch to my uncles. He threw lightning. He stood in our alfalfa field firing the ball like I'd never seen a grown man do up close.

My uncle caught and remarked, "Hot almighty, I think that fool broke my damn hand."

The only time I ever saw him compete was when he pitched part of an impromptu home-run derby during a Methodist barbecue.

Older men in the bleachers mumbled to themselves, "You know Dietrich could throw like that?"

"No," another Methodist remarked. "I'd'a never guessed."

Yeah. Me neither.

They hoarded around him afterward. They asked a million questions. He didn't give them much in the way of answers. I think they embarrassed him.

Anyway, the World Series ended at midnight. It was quite a game. An extra inning. Heart murmurs. Players swarming the field in droves. Jumping. Embracing. Pointing to the sky. One player held his father so tight he almost suffocated him.

You've never seen so many grown men cry. Some, because of baseball.

Others because of ghosts.

Eight to seven. Cubs.

A MOTHER'S LOVE

She took my vitals in the exam room. She was in her sixties. Rough skin, a laugh that sounded like unfiltered Camels.

She unstrapped my Velcro cuff and said my blood pressure was good.

Then she high-fived me.

"So," she said. "You got foot problems, huh? I got bad feet, too. You must work long hours."

Not really.

I've been lucky. Men like my daddy worked long hours. My grandfather: self-flagellated.

She's a lot like them. She's worked since age ten. At this stage, she's supposed to be enjoying the easy life. It's not working out.

"I moved to the beach to relax," she said. "But I don't get to. Too busy working."

Her daughter is in her mid-twenties. She was born with the umbilical cord wrapped around her neck. It made her slow. If that's not enough, the girl also has heart trouble—undergoing open heart surgery twice. She is also half deaf.

Life hasn't exactly been hopscotch.

"I've prayed a lot," she said, "When she was a baby, I'd say, 'God, if you want Rachel to live, she will.' He must've known I needed her."

Must have.

Times were tight. She worked as a mail carrier in middle Georgia to make ends meet. Then, a friend suggested she get a job as a medical tech.

"I worked at Emory for years," she said. "Loved it. It helped us get ahead, moneywise."

And then, a vacation to the beach changed everything. Nowhere before had the two felt so at home.

"My daughter was like, 'Mom! I wanna live here, it's so beautiful!'"

So, she sent out resumes. She got a job half a mile from the Gulf. Life was still hard, but at least now it was pretty, too.

"High school was a challenge," she said. "College was worse. She has to work harder than you'n me. Sometimes I wanted to intervene. But, I knew she needed to learn to stand on her own feet."

Her daughter just finished college last year. She's an English major. To celebrate, they took a cruise to Mexico. The girl brought along her new boyfriend.

"My daughter thinks he might be the ONE."

She showed me cellphone images of a lanky girl and boy. They wore bathing suits and held drinks with little umbrellas. Goofy smiles.

"Lord knows," she said. "Rachel needs somebody who's prepared to care for her. I won't be around forever."

She laughed.

"I don't know what I'm gonna do when my baby leaves, she's been my whole life."

Well, I don't know what you'll do, ma'am. But I do know one thing.

It's time to get off those aching feet.

And go to the beach.

A MAN IN TOWN

His biological father beat his mother. But after eight years of busted cheekbones, she hit the road. In the middle of the night, she and her four kids left.

It took two days to drive from Tennessee to Alabama.

"Mama was from the old world," he said. "Didn't even know how to drive. So I drove the whole way."

He was thirteen. He sat atop suitcases and pressed the pedal with his tip-toes. When his younger siblings got fidgety, he pulled over so everyone could make water.

It was a new town. They were foreigners. They moved into a drafty farmhouse with cheap rent. She took a waitress job. He worked at a hardware store after school.

Once, he remembers not having enough to pay the power bill. They went without lightbulbs for six months. If you've ever wanted to hear about hard living, he's your man.

"Folks didn't like Mama," he goes on. "Especially other women. It was a different time. In a small town, a single pretty girl, with kids... People talked about her."

One day, a man in town stopped by the restaurant. She was on shift. He was taken with her. He tipped two fifty-dollar bills, leaving them under his plate.

When she saw the money her temper flared. She

stormed over to his house to give it back.

"I don't need no charity from nobody," she insisted.

Skull of iron, that woman.

So, the man offered to pay her to clean his house on Saturdays. It made good sense. He was a bachelor, she'd been skipping suppers to save on groceries. She accepted.

He overpaid.

They became friends. One thing led to another. He asked her out to movies, picnics, church socials, lunch dates. People gossiped—said they were mismatched. Maybe they were.

Then it happened. The man didn't get down on his knee to ask—after all, they weren't kids anymore. She said yes.

"Mama went from poor little waitress, to happy," he said. "All because of a good man. That's why we never called him stepfather, we called him, Dad."

And a father he was. When he died, his adopted kids cried harder than anyone. His funeral was one of the biggest in the county.

You can tell a lot about a man by his last service.

"Mama was a mess," he went on. "But when I saw him in the casket, I decided right then, I was gonna follow in his shoes and go into the family business."

That was ages ago. He's practically an old man now. White hair and all.

But now you know why he's a preacher.

FOR SPACIOUS SKIES

Once, I saw an old man stumble on the curb. It happened outside a Mexican restaurant. He fell hard and cut himself. A waitress ran to help. He was bleeding on the pavement.

"First-aid kit!" she yelled.

He had a gash. She stitched him up with a needle and thread.

"Where'd you learn to do that?" the man asked.

"I was an Army medic," she said. "Used to practice on tomatoes all the time."

When she finished, he embraced her and got blood all over her shirt. He cried. She didn't.

Army girls.

Listen, I don't care how many election signs pepper the landscape. I don't care how many horrid disagreements there are. I love this country. Every bit of it. The good, the bad, and the Army medics.

I also love single mothers. The young man who unloads trucks at Winn Dixie. The woman standing outside the hair salon, smoking. The kids holding bake-sales for breast cancer. And anyone strong enough to go down swinging.

Tracy—who got out of jail a few weeks ago. She saw her kids for the first time in two long years.

Arnold, my pal who left his fancy marketing job to drive a semi. His wife goes with him. He sent me postcards from the Grand Canyon. They just found out his wife is pregnant.

I like Pat, who wants to be a welding teacher. The supermarket employee with Downs syndrome who told me, "You have a colorful face, sir."

Nobody's ever told me that before.

I like Roger—wounded Afghanistan veteran with mangled hands. Who said, "My therapist says I need to start living my life. So, I'm learning guitar."

You beat all, Roger.

I love Minette, whose husband is in critical condition. I love the South American woman who dug through her purse for exact change.

I love the man who paid for my lunch. I don't know him, but he told me to, "Have a blessed day."

Blessed.

Yeah, well, I am blessed. Not because of what I own, but because of where I am. This country is part of me. It's where my great grandparents were born. Where I was baptized.

It's not a place made of mountains and prairies. It's people. Common folks. Fishermen, guitar players, and medics. People who believe in something so big they string up flags and sing about it.

Go ahead, fuss and fight over who wins the election. I don't give a damn how hard the folks in business suits try to tear us apart. It won't work. It can't work. Because we are still one nation. Under God.

Indivisible.

And even if they do rip us to shreds...

I know an Army medic who's hell with a needle and thread.

HAPPY BOY

He was a happy kid. He grew up with nothing, out in the sticks. His daddy was a turpentiner. His mother was a baby-machine. He had marvelous tales about the old days.

But they were nothing compared to his best story, about how he died—twice. He told that one often. Especially around redheaded freckle-faces.

It went like this:

While in his forties, on the operating table, he died. Three whole minutes. Doctors thought he was a goner. He came back. Then it happened again.

"Heaven is real," he told me once. "I seen it with my own eyes. And you know what I learnt? The secret."

My eyes were the size of tractor rims.

He asked if I wanted to learn it. I didn't even have to think. You bet your cotton balls I did.

"Come here," he said. "I'll show you."

He wrapped his arms around me so hard I heard my ribs creak. He held me that way for two minutes. No words. He smelled like cigarettes and Old Spice.

"THAT'S the secret," he said. "And that's how you change the world."

Oh.

Despite his poverty-stricken upbringing, he was jolly

enough to make Santa look like a jerk.

He knew funny songs, complicated jokes, and he was bad to cry when the spirit hit him. Like when he talked about his mother. Or: when he talked about how he met his wife as a teenager—at a rat killing party.

Later in life, he worked as a salesman to keep his family fed. He sold everything from life insurance, to turkeys and vacuums.

"Vacuums was the worst," he once said. "Had to lug'em to doorsteps before you even knocked. It was something awful, but you'll do anything to feed your young'uns."

He smoked like a fish and talked a purple streak. If you were lucky enough to catch him on smoke break, you'd see him do both.

I got an email yesterday.

It was his daughter. A heart attack. He wasn't even supposed to live this long. He was nearly a hundred. I suppose happy things generally last longer than miserable ones.

His daughter went on to say that, in the end, he'd become tender. He got so he couldn't watch the news without crying. They had to unplug his televisions.

His daughter brought the grandkids to see him before he passed. He couldn't do magic tricks with his stiff hands, and his stories were hard to follow since his last stroke.

But she overheard him asking one of the boys if he wanted to know the secret to life.

The kid said yes.

So, he showed him how to change the world.

BEAUTIFUL FAILURES

Waffle House—my waitress is named Laura. I know this because it's on her name-tag. She's worked three shifts, back-to-back. Her eyes are sagging.

Laura has four kids. Three boys, one girl. She shows me photos on her phone.

"That's my oldest," she says, tapping the screen. "She's got a brain. I hope she makes more outta her life than I ever did. "

She smiles. Her teeth are a wreck. She's gorgeous.

"What's so bad about your life?" I ask.

"Nothing, but I know I'm a failure, I'm okay with that."

Well, I'll be dog.

I've known some failures in my time. Laura's not one. Her hands might be rough and she might not descend from blue bloodlines, but she's not trash.

If she is, then I'm a club member.

After all, my family isn't exactly showroom material. My father wore denim. My mother lived in a trailer. I've owned four myself. Three leaked. One resides in the county dump.

And, my education is minimal. I went to college on my own dime and did miserably, working grunt labor in the daytime.

When I passed my final, I walked outside and shouted in the parking lot—it seemed appropriate. A few classmates were outside smoking. A man with a tattoo on his neck offered me a cigarette.

"I don't smoke," I said.

"Neither do I," he answered. "But we just graduated, that's a big deal for people like you'n me."

You and me.

He was right. It was a big deal. As a boy, my mother sewed my clothes and shopped at thrift stores. Sometimes she even recycled teabags.

Then there was the time in eighth grade when a girl called me white trash. Her name was Beth. I'll never forget her.

"Your shirt has a hole," she pointed out, then mumbled the ugly phrase.

It surprised me. Until that day, I'd never considered myself so lowly. I threw the shirt away and bawled like a fool. I still think about her sometimes.

Some things stick with you.

Anyway, I left a healthy tip for Laura. Not because I feel sorry for her—I don't.

I feel no sympathy for failures who wake at three to make breakfast for screaming kids, then work twenty-four hours. Neither do I feel sorry for losers who pay the rent. Nor for low-class kids who wear thrift-store shirts with holes in them.

I do not feel a drop of pity because you don't pity the strong. And though it might not mean much coming from me, I hope Laura's reading this now.

If she is, listen up:

I'm proud of you, Laura. Proud as hell.

Now you say it.

GIVE THANKS

My uncle deep fried a turkey. At age twelve, I'd never seen such a thing. He claimed it made the bird taste better.

But I think he did it because he liked sipping Budweiser outdoors.

It was my first Thanksgiving as a fatherless kid. It was going to be a lonely one. The holidays seemed to make happy people happier, and sad people more lonely. Even our dog was sad.

Daddy's Lab had gotten into a trash bag of his old clothes and made a bed out of his button-downs. I guess she wanted to smell him.

When someone dies. You empty their closet and fill storage bags with their clothes. It's the worst chore you'll ever do. But it's better than looking at orphaned hanging clothes.

My uncle lifted the turkey from the peanut oil.

"Needs more time," he said.

I visited the kitchen. My aunt was preparing a humble meal. Potatoes, greens, sweet potato pie, gravy.

In the den, Mama sat on the sofa, staring out the window. She didn't have much to say. In fact, she hadn't said more than a few words in months.

A knock on the door.

Mama made a face, saying, "We're not expecting company."

It was my cousins. They brought squash casserole. Mama forced a fake smile. So did I.

Another knock. My aunt and uncle—with chicken gizzards.

More knocks. Two more uncles, two more aunts. They brought cheese straws.

Doorbell.

The Millers, McLanes, and Jacksons from church. They'd brought an entire bakery and fourteen rugrats.

Knock, knock, knock.

Dan and Meredith, from the farm behind us. They'd brought a bathtub-cooler of Coke and beer. More knocks. Three members of my ball team, sporting neckties and greased hair.

Then:

Mister Dole and his wife. They brought venison back strap, boiled peanuts, and his hunting dog.

Daddy's friend Billy—holding a plastic milk-jug of something clear.

Miss Wanda, with tomato relish, pickled okra, poundcake, and her magnificent husband, Harry.

Mister Don brought me a copy of Field and Stream.

My buddy Ryan and his grandma brought potato salad, pear salad, god-awful tomato aspic.

There were so many people in our house, it sounded like a flock of flamingos. Not a single frown, nor a hand without an aluminum can. Women crowded the kitchen. Men sat out back, smoking, telling illicit jokes.

And for the first time, even if only for a few hours, I smiled.

When it was time to say grace, everyone congregated, spilling out of the kitchen. Elbow to elbow.

"Dear God," my uncle began, removing his cap. "May we never forget the true reason we've gathered

together here today."
 Well, there's no way we could.
 Not ever.
 You don't forget deep fried turkey.

HUMAN BEINGS

Atlanta, Georgia—once, I took my friend to the ER after he broke his ankle running a 5K. The young man in the hospital room beside us was suffering from a gunshot.

His mother sat with him. She was small, gray-headed. She did not cry, nor raise her voice. She whispered while nurses and police officers hurried around him.

He kept mumbling, "I'm sorry, Mama."

She gave one long, "*Sssssssshhhhhh*," then said, "You're my baby boy."

When they wheeled him to surgery, she lost it. Nurses could barely hold her up. I've never seen a woman scream like that.

Not ever.

Panama City, Florida—I saw a truck crash into a neighborhood telephone pole. It happened during broad daylight.

A police officer lived a few houses away from the accident. He heard the loud sound. There were sparks. Buzzing. The power went out.

The deputy tore out the front door, jogging barefoot. He pulled the dazed kid from the truck and held him. A crowd of neighbors gathered.

The deputy cradled the boy, saying, "It's alright, son."

Mobile, Alabama—I watched a toddler have a meltdown in the supermarket. He sat on the floor wailing. His mother tried to console him.

An elderly woman calmed the boy. She used a Snicker's as her weapon of choice.

The mother said, "We adopted him a week ago. He's our first, and I don't think he likes us." She started sobbing.

The older lady wrote her number on the back of a card and said, "I've raised two boys. You're gonna be fine. Call me."

I hope she did.

Pensacola, Florida—Boy Scouts held a car wash on the side of the road. My wife and I pulled over. She let them give our vehicle the once-over for fifteen bucks.

I asked why they were raising money.

"Because," one boy said. "My mom has breast cancer. She's not doing good."

When they finished, my wife paid them for two more cleanings.

I left the tip.

Right now, I can't sleep. I'm writing this because the world's gone haywire. All you have to do is peek outside to see. Or flip on the television. Hate is for sale, and it's flying off the shelves.

It's too bad. Because this world's a lot damned bigger than a TV screen. And since you've read this far, I've got something I want to say:

If you're an off-duty deputy with a big heart, a mother who doesn't know what she's doing, an abandoned child, a newlywed, a dog lover, cat lover, a Boy Scout with a sick mother, a gray-haired mama with the strength of ten thousand angels.

Or a human being.

God bless you.

MAMA TRIED

"I won't have you turning my son into a preacher," his father once shouted to his mother, during an argument.

To men like his father, there was nothing worse than a soft-handed Bible-man, stuck in an office. He wanted his boy to do what men have done since the dawn of testosterone—spit, cuss, grow callouses.

His mother wanted him to memorize the Sermon on the Mount.

So, the kid tried to do both. He attended Sunday school, learned the Bible, recited long passages from memory. Outside of church, he worked with his father, operating heavy machinery, learning to cuss.

He was a rowdy child. He drank too much, smoked more, and hopped from party to party. Since he discovered long ago he couldn't please both parents, he disappointed them instead.

He was successful at that.

He was in the car with his friends when the cops pulled them over. A routine traffic stop. One of the boys had just robbed a grocery store and had a gun tucked in his jacket. Another boy had meth in his pocket.

Off to prison.

That's where he met Billy, who runs an educational

program, teaching inmates to read and write poetry and literature.

Billy says, "It helps'em work through their emotional stuff. You wouldn't believe some of the things these boys write. Ain't a dry eye in the classroom sometimes."

For his first project, he wrote nothing. Instead, he recited something he learned long ago.

"I couldn't believe he knew the whole Sermon on the Mount from start to finish," Billy says. "There was something exceptional about him."

Billy took special interest in the kid. It only took a few heart-to-heart conversations for the kid to realize what he wanted to do with his life.

He wanted to make his mother proud.

"See" Billy explains. "Lotta these boys ain't bad, just mixed up."

With Billy's help, the boy finished a GED. When he completed that, Billy enrolled him in an online Bible college—which cost a lot.

"Someone in my church funded him," said Billy, winking at me. "Anonymous sponsor."

Right.

By the time the kid got out of prison, he'd already baptized handfuls of inmates, and led church services. During each service, Billy stood on the sidelines, prouder than a parent.

Billy goes on, "The guys all listened to him. I think they thought, 'Hey, he's kinda like me, if he can do it, why can't I?' Yeah, I think he found his calling."

Billy laughs.

"Hell, he's made more of a difference in here than I ever have."

Sorry to point it out to you, Billy.

But you're wrong about that.

STORY MAN

He was good with a joke. Real good.

Each Thanksgiving or Christmas, he had a pocketful of zingers. All the men in the family would gather in the den after supper just to hear the racy ones.

The boys did, too.

"It was his thing," says the grandson. "Sometimes, his jokes were so good, we didn't know whether to laugh or clap."

His sense of humor came from a childhood spent during the darkest days of American history. When the boll weevil, the stock market, and war ruined the world.

One Thanksgiving, the grandson tells me the old man surprised everyone.

"He had no jokes," the grandson says. "He had a story about his life. We didn't expect it from a jokester like him. But you could tell he thought it was important."

It was. After all, the man came from an era when things like storytelling and guitar picking were thought to be important. When front porches and living rooms were more valuable than, say, twenty-four-hour news networks.

That holiday, the old man sat, feet propped up, sipping corn liquor—which the doctor expressly warned against. The redder his cheeks got, the easier his memory ran.

He described a lonely childhood after his father's death. About how his daddy died from bee stings—they swarmed him in the woods. It was a freak accident.

He talked about being so poor he shoveled manure for pennies. How suppers consisted of ketchup and water —they called it tomato soup. About stealing chickens from nearby farms to keep from starving. About singing in the living room to keep from complaining.

"It was sobering," the grandson recounts. "None of us knew these things about him. Nobody dared interrupt him."

The old man spoke of pumping gas when fuel was cheaper than Coke. He talked about country dances, where boys behaved like men. And girls expected them to. About the magic of a fiddle.

He talked about her—whose photograph stayed in his breast pocket while he was in Europe. About the War, Germans, watching nineteen-year-olds die, and the bullet in his armpit.

About hell on earth, hard work, family sacrifice, and how much fun he'd had doing it all.

When he finished, the den fell silent. A few people sniffled. Someone finally broke the silence, saying, "How about some poundcake?"

A sure fire way to empty a room.

The den cleared out except for one grandson. The boy sat criss-cross on the floor, asking the old man for more.

"More?" The man just shook his head. "In the name of God, boy. You'd rather hear old-man stories than eat cake? You're just like your dummy grandaddy. You poor damn soul."

It was his last Thanksgiving.

I am that poor damn soul.

I'M A FEEDER

Her husband died of prostate cancer. She grieved long and hard. People worried she'd never get over it. She told my aunt she didn't want to get over it.

So she didn't.

Not until the fateful day she went grocery shopping and noticed the homeless folks begging at a busy Atlanta intersection—a popular corner among people looking for handouts.

She'd ignored them in times past, like most do. But something touched her. It was an ordinary-looking man and his son.

He held a cardboard sign, reading: "Son is hungry."

She drove by. Then, regret overwhelmed her. She turned around and put twenty bucks in his hand. If she would've had more, she would've given it.

"I couldn't bear to think that boy was going hungry," she said.

She saw him a few days later. She gave more. And that's when the Mama Bear in her awakened. They were feelings she hadn't felt since her husband died.

"I'm a feeder," she told me. "And I knew they weren't eating real, hot food."

This would never do.

She went home and rediscovered her apron. She

cooked things like casseroles in foil dishes—and cornbread. It was the first time she'd used her kitchen since her husband.

The next day, she went to the intersection but didn't see the man nor his son. Instead, it was a young woman asking for cash.

"The food was still hot," she said. "So I gave it to her. You should'a seen her face. Was like I gave her gold."

Gold.

She returned to her kitchen. Twice as many foil dishes. Twice the cornbread.

Again she visited. No man. No son. This time, it was an older gentleman with girlfriend and a Labrador. She gave them paper bags. They God-blessed her.

She God-blessed back.

It wasn't long before her church friends got in on the action. A handful of ladies cooked every Wednesday.

Soon, they were opening the fellowship hall doors to under-privileged kids, out of work parents, elderly folks, and anyone who liked cornbread that wasn't from a box.

She did this twenty-two years.

"I believe that man and his son were angels," she said. "If it wasn't for them, I'd never have realized my purpose. I'd still be a lonely old widow."

She doesn't cook anymore. She lives in a rest home, one with a cafeteria that sits only feet from her bedroom —she tells me the cornbread is mediocre at best. She has her own nurse. She's not lonely.

I asked how many people she thinks she's fed over the years.

She looked me in the eyes and said, "Not enough. Not nearly enough. How about you?"

Ditto.

GRATEFUL BOYS

I am on my porch, sitting. The sun is setting. Linus, former feral cat and rodent security patrol, is toying with a mouse. He's holding it by the tail.

Poor rat.

Two neighbor kids ride bikes down my gravel road. They see me. And since childhood knows no privacy, they march up my steps, uninvited. Heavy breathing.

The conversation drifts toward Thanksgiving. Their teacher has assigned writing homework. They're supposed to list things they're thankful for. They're stuck.

"You're over thinking it," I suggest. "Try starting with little things. Like GI Joe dolls."

"What's GI Joe?" one asks.

God help us.

"What are YOU thankful for, Mister Sean?"

Well, it bears mentioning, I am thankful for lots. Namely: biscuits. The kind cooked in skillets. Sometimes, I think I write too much about biscuits.

I'm also grateful for baskets of pine cones. The cones on our cofee table smell like cinnamon. My wife bought them at Walmart for a buck.

A buck.

I'm grateful for the fish I caught. After an

unsuccessful day, I tried one last cast. I snagged a trout the size of a baby cucumber. Not large enough to eat. Big enough to lie about.

Feather pillows, I'm grateful for those. Synthetic foam is a joke.

I like sunny days so bright they make you tired. Black and white movies. Roy Rogers, Gene Autry, and John Wayne.

"Who're they?" the kids ask.

Somebody, please save America's youth.

I'm grateful for Baptist hymnals. I have one dated, 1928. Sometimes I thumb through it. And for Daddy's old guitar. The finish has worn off, it looks like hell, but old hymns sound nice on it.

For the mountains in Tennessee, North Carolina, Georgia, and North Alabama. God lives up there. For our soggy marshes in North Florida—his summer cottage is here.

For the creek behind my house. For the fort I found while walking through the woods—it was made of old plywood. I'm glad kids still build forts.

I'm grateful to be on this porch instead of ICU. I have a friend who died just last night. He had a good life. I'm sorry his wife had to make the god-awful decision to unplug him. I'm sorry his kids will grow up hating Father's Day.

We weren't close. But I'm grateful I knew him as a boy.

I'm grateful for boys. Little fellas who play hard, who catch frogs, who own puppies, and think they'll live forever. Who still cry when they get hurt. Who don't know sorrow—or hate. Who call me Mister Sean, and make me sorry the stork has passed me by.

But most of all,

I'm grateful for GI Joe dolls.

LOVE STORY

Betty met her husband when she was eighteen. He was playing the guitar at a party. It was the kind of shindig your grandparents went to. Girls in cotton dresses, rough-handed boys, and sawdust floors.

"He was scrawny as you please," she said. "Could sing like a bird."

She had to have him.

When he put the instrument down, she made a beeline for him. He was nervous. He avoided her. It boiled her blood. Betty wasn't about to let Bean-Pole get away.

During their first conversation, she found that he stammered. Badly.

It was his lifelong affliction. He'd tried joining the military, they rejected him. School was even worse. He could hardly spell his own name. Uttering a sentence was like delivering puppies.

But when he sang, words came easy.

They dated. He sang to her. She helped him learn to read. They studied late nights in his mother's kitchen, burning cigarettes, reading grade-school textbooks.

He wanted to lose his impediment. For her.

"He went to the preacher for prayer," she said. "But it didn't work. He finally gave up. I just told him, it doesn't matter, John. I'd love you even if you were deaf and dumb."

Love him she did.

At nineteen, they got married at the Justice of the Peace's house. It was Christmas Eve night. He had a few days off from the pulp mill. They did what they could.

"He borrowed his brother's dress suit," she went on. "It was too big, he was so handsome."

She wore her nicest dress—white with yellow flowers. Their knees shook when they said their vows. For a gift, he bought her chocolate. As it turned out, she bought him the same thing.

Theirs was an ordinary love. The kind easily missed by the restless. Some folks are so busy looking for nuclear explosions, they miss out on a good campfire.

She says he kissed her often. He was known to surprise her with little gifts. He'd hide them under her pillow, or in the cupboard. He knew how to make her laugh.

They just celebrated their anniversary last Christmas. Their children rented a small banquet hall and threw a real party. They even hired a band.

He was old, but not too far gone. He borrowed a guitar. He played, "You Are My Sunshine."

He never took his eyes off the lady in the front. His voice wasn't as steady as it once was. People clapped. Betty cried.

He's gone now. Not forgotten.

"If you decide to write about John," she said. "You gotta write the whole thing as a love story, because that's what we were. We were a love story."

Yes, ma'am.

Sixty-nine years of marriage. I guess you were.

I'LL FLY AWAY

I know. It's only a wristwatch. Even the jeweler says it's worthless. I've sent it off, paid four hundred bucks. They took it apart, replaced gears.

Nothing.

I don't know why I wear it. My father's watch is dead weight.

You have no reason to care about this, but my daddy wanted to be a pilot since childhood. When folks asked the redhead what he wanted to be, he gave the same four-word answer.

"I wanna fly airplanes."

By high school it was a five-word answer. "I'm gonna fly Navy planes."

Truth told, that's hard for me to imagine—Daddy with such youthful ambition. The only man I ever knew was a steelworker who sweat buckets for a pittance and rode tractors after work.

He could make dead trucks run, hum every hymn, and strike an arc with the best stick-welder.

He was no pilot.

As a young man, Daddy signed up to take the Navy aviation physical exam. The smooth-faced version of my father sat in the waiting room, knees bouncing.

I'll bet he glanced at this very wristwatch every

couple seconds. Because on that day, this thing would've been brand new. He paid a lot for it. It's an aviator's timepiece.

The Navy doctor checked his vision. Daddy had hawk eyes.

The next exam: his ears. My father was deaf on his left side. It took ninety seconds for the doc to show him the door.

He stood outside on the sidewalk. I don't know whether he cried, but I do know he threw his new watch on the pavement.

And that was the end. My father was landlocked. No one would ever know him as anything but a dirty-faced welder. Including his own boy.

I remember a family get-together. My cousin brought a young man she was dating. Blonde kid.

A Navy pilot.

He and Daddy talked until the wee hours. They sat on the back porch. He asked the young man what flying was like.

The kid said it was indescribable.

It made Daddy smile. Not a happy grin, but the kind you give at funerals.

Then, the kid said something else to Daddy.

Daddy cocked his good ear toward him. "Say again, son?"

The kid repeated, "I said, nice watch."

Daddy shook it and listened to it.

For the life of me, I don't know why he wore that broken thing. Maybe because people can love dead things just as much as living ones. Or, perhaps it reminded him of youth. Of how bad he'd always wanted to fly.

And that's why I wear it.

Because some glad morning he finally did.

FRYING CHICKENS

North Carolina—I'm looking at Purple Mountains Majesty. The autumn here is so colorful it's heart-stopping.

Today, I drove through the Smokies. My wife wanted a live chicken for our Thanksgiving vacation. She's hellbent on it. She found a farm on Craigslist, located an hour's drive from our cabin.

And since I have nothing better to do than fish, she sent me across state lines.

After a scenic drive on Highway 74, I found myself in a small community where locals pronounce the word tire as "tar," and have brown spit.

My wife arranged for me to meet a chicken farmer at the Chevron station.

Her name was Wanda, and she is pure mountain. I couldn't tell how old she was. Her skin is rawhide, her hair is snow.

I followed her Jeep through ten miles of dirt. Her homestead consisted of two shacks and a barn, which sat on a sprawling automobile graveyard. This is a place where Chevys, Fords, and pickups go to die.

"What's with the cars?" I asked.

"My paw used to be in the scrapyard business."

Then, Wanda led me to a series of coops where I selected a plump-looking red bird. She told me the hen's name was Barbara. She charged me thirty bucks for

Barbara—which is highway robbery—then handed me an axe.

"You wanna do it?" she said. "Or you want me?"

I'm no stranger to poultry sacrifice. As a boy, we raised chickens. Once, a catering company called us for fifty-four birds. It took me two hours to kill them all, four hours to prep them, a day to clean the aftermath.

Wanda did the honors. She introduced Barbara to Our Savior, then cleaned the carcass on a plastic table.

"You like music?" Wanda asked.

"Sure."

"Well, you oughta come eat at my church, Thanksgiving. It's free, we got music."

Wanda explained that her church opens its doors for all God's children to sample the best covered dishes in the county. She plays string bass in the band.

"'Lotta poor folks up here," she says, plucking feathers. "We try to feed folks that need help. Good food, board games, singin', it's fun."

She wraps Barbara's remains in brown paper.

"First time I went, my daughter took me for Christmas supper. Back then, I was a worthless drunk, everyone knew it. Lost my kids, my husband... That church, they treated me like I's family."

It's been a long time since Wanda's touched a bottle. And she's been telling people about how she saw the light ever since. In fact, she gave me a rundown on how I, too, might find salvation—in case I was looking for it.

She said, "I just try to spread the Good News to anyone who might not know. I mean, 'cause I'd be nothing without the grace from..."

She points up.

Before I leave, I hug Wanda's neck. Not for the chicken.

But because I know where she's pointing.

HOW TO LOVE A WOMAN

Girls like flowers, so buy her flowers. It's that simple. You're fifteen, she's fifteen. Not enough fifteen-year-olds give flowers anymore.

When I was fifteen, my uncle once sent my aunt flowers. It was like the Second Coming took place on the porch.

My aunt told me, "Lotta problems could be solved if boys bought flowers now and then."

I'm inclined to agree. I know bouquets get a bad reputation among fellas your age,—which is a shame— but these boys are missing out.

There's nothing more exhilarating than standing on a doorstep, wondering if she'll like zinnias, if she'll like you, or whether her father has violent tendencies.

Also, I feel obliged to tell you, this new girlfriend isn't just a girl. This is a human.

The problem, of course, is that each underwear ad, swimsuit magazine, and perfume commercial is trying to make her into something else.

This world has done women wrong. It's ruined their confidence. It expects them to be scholars, nannies, interior decorators, chefs, maids, and ER nurses. It tells them to be leaner, tanner, taller, slimmer, faster, trendier, sleeker, and blonder.

And if that doesn't break your heart, let me tell you about the sixteen-year-old whose boyfriend told her she was fat.

He made fun of her. She went on a diet. Dyed her hair. She eventually lost a few sizes, then she had a few bouts with anorexia. It was bad. She's in therapy now.

I'm no expert, but she didn't need carb-counting. She needed flowers.

I guess what I'm trying to say is: I know you're only a kid, but I'm counting on you to save the world.

Long ago, our ancestors gave us a society with country dances, fiddle bands, and walks home after dark. We ruined it. We traded the whole thing in for rock music that sounds like angry chainsaws, and mass shootings.

Listen, this is about more than proms, holding hands, snuggling, and whatever else fifteen-year-olds do. This is about something big. In fact, it's the most important thing of all time.

It's about learning to be unselfish, unconditional, and understanding. How to be wrong, and how to admit it.

It's about seeing a person with your eyes closed. About opening doors for anyone you'd call ma'am, miss, or Mama. About decency.

This is love, kid. Not just romance. It's bigger than that. I'm talking about the sort that could change the universe. I wish I could tell you more about it, but I'm still learning.

Though there is one thing I can say with certainty.

Buy her flowers.

WORRY

I'm not a physician, but I'm about as close as you can get. And as a highly trained liberal arts major, I'd like to give you a prescription.

Don't worry.

Don't make me say it twice.

Of course, I shouldn't suggest such a thing. Trying to quit worrying is like trying to keep a pet squirrel.

I once had a pet squirrel—I'm not making this up—named Hank Williams Aaron. One day, I opened the cage to feed him. All I saw was a brown blur. Hank was halfway to Galveston before I could say his name.

My point: you can't stop worrying. Because your mind is like a squirrel, the moment you open the door, it goes nuts, so to speak.

I don't even know what I'm saying here.

The truth is, I was going to write about something else. But today, I saw a young girl crying outside the doctor's office. It got to me.

She sat on a bench, head hung low. A puddle in her lap. People walked by, uninterested.

An old woman finally stopped and hugged the girl.

They exchanged no words. Only painful smiles.

Look, I know life isn't fair. In fact it's downright criminal. Flat tires, red bank accounts, relationship disasters, a bad diagnosis, busted bones. Death. I don't know what fate dumped in your lap, but I know it stinks.

You have a right to worry, you're a person. This world kicks you in the teeth, then steals your wallet. What kind of idiot would tell you not to worry?

Me.

Yesterday, I pulled out old photos. I thumbed through and saw images of my ancestors. They were poor. I'm talking lucky-to-make-it-past-forty poor.

Then, I found a few pictures of myself, awkward boy that I used to be. Chubby faced, freckled. That kid had a lot to learn—just like his poor ancestors did before him.

And it wasn't all hopscotch and ping pong, either. You and I have learned the kinds of lessons that left us bleeding on the pavement.

So, even though I don't know you from Adam's older sister, I do know a little something about you. The things you've endured have made you, you. And you wouldn't trade them for all the squirrels in Galveston.

I also know that these few paragraphs aren't going to make a damn bit of difference in your life. But since you've read this far, I guess I want to say something.

It doesn't matter what happens today, how dark the sky, or how bad you think it is.

I love you.

And it's going to be all right.

THE SOUTH

I'm driving. I see old barns outside my window. I counted three in the time it took me to write that.

Also: I see cattle. Pastures—brown from fall weather. A bright sky. An old billboard that reads: "Sinners go to hell."

Another billboard: "I buy junk, but sell antiques."

I pulled over to visit this junk shop, which was once an old service station. Because shopping for garbage is my favorite pastime.

The old woman behind the counter has silver hair that hangs down to her hips.

"Anything in 'ticular you huntin', hon?"

"You got any old pocket knives?"

"'Course we got'em. 'Ere's a passel of'em rye chonder."

I'll bet they don't have passels up north.

This two-lane highway is more or less empty today. It's a weekend, and people are spending time at family homesteads. That's how things go in this part of the world. Family first. Family second. Family last.

We pass several houses with herds of cars parked out front. These are old, single-story homes you don't usually notice when you ride by. They have plank-siding, tin roofs, screen doors, live oaks in the front, tire swings.

I haven't seen a good tire swing in ages.

My father hung tire swings often. Once, he scaled to the top of an oak to hang one from high branches. He climbed better than any of my pals.

"How'd you learn to climb like that?" one kid asked.

"I'm an iron-worker, son," said Daddy. "We can climb anything."

The boys were impressed.

Well, I'll bet he couldn't have climbed these trees I'm driving past now. These things are covered in kudzu. You can't climb anything covered in that. I have tried.

My aunt's backyard was a kudzu jungle. I decided to conquer one of these trees. And, since I was the son of an iron-worker, I believed genetics were on my side. They weren't.

Just now, a semi-truck shot by me. He has the rebel flag flying on his radio antenna. He gave me the stink-eye. He thinks I'm driving too slow.

Maybe I am. I don't like to be in a hurry when I go this way. I enjoy this route too much—which cuts through Georgia, Alabama, and the Panhandle.

I like to watch the trees change from fat ones to skinny longleafs. These are the same kinds of pines that surround our bay.

The north side of the bay is where I learned to drive a boat. Where I caught my first redfish. Where you can hunt duck, spikes, coons, and mullet.

Now I'm on my street.

There's my house. The grass is long, my siding is moldy in some spots. Over in the tall weeds sits my boat.

At the window is my coonhound. She's howling, turning circles, slobbering on the glass.

Some folks travel the world over. I never have. Even though it's none of my business, I suspect they're looking for their own heaven.

I hope they find it.

I just drove through mine.

HAND IN HAND

She is old. And she tells a story of the old days. Back when the world was a different place. Electricity was a luxury. Suppers were cooked on iron stoves. Men tipped hats to ladies.

Things have changed.

She was a nice-looking child. I saw the photo that proves it. Big smile. Blonde curls. And like three quarters of Alabama at the time, she lived on the rural route.

As a young girl, her morning routine was feeding chickens, then helping her mother fix breakfast. She'd run outside, climb over the chicken fence, and gather eggs. Her mother warned her not to scale the tall fence, but nine-year-olds do not listen.

One morning, she fell from the top. Her fingers got caught in the chicken wire. It was serious and bloody. She lost two fingers and severed a tendon in her thumb.

Throughout childhood, she became good at hiding her mangled hand. Often, she kept a fist to conceal her missing parts. When she got old enough to like boys, they did not return the favor.

One year, her high school threw a Sadie Hawkins dance—where girls invite fellas. She cooked up enough courage to ask a boy. He turned her down. So she tried another. Same response. No takers.

That hurt.

Life went on. When she was in her twenties, she accompanied her father to the hardware store—a place men lingered to talk gossip. It was a pleasant porch, covered in brown spit.

That's where she met him. He was sitting with the others. He rose to his feet when he saw her. He was eleven years her senior. A war veteran. Tall. Skinny. Sandy hair.

She kept her hands in her dress pockets.

He smiled at her. She smiled back. That weekend, he called on her—and in those days that meant calling her father.

He picked her up. They took in a movie. He gave her royal treatment. He was no boy, but a man. Different from others. Decent to a fault.

A few weeks after she met him, she'd worked up enough bravery to show him her damaged hand. She was certain he'd be repulsed and lose interest.

She showed it to him anyway.

He just shrugged and told her how beautiful she was.

She insisted to know whether her hand bothered him.

He didn't answer. Instead, he told her about the War. About the winter his unit got captured. About almost freezing to death in a prison camp. About the frostbite he endured.

Then he removed his boot and showed her his missing toes.

When she finished, I asked whether her story was true.

She says people ask that all the time.

WHISKEY AND CAMELS

Pensacola, Florida—it's raining. Hard. I wish I had a few bucks to give the man standing at the stop sign. He goes from car to car, holding an open stocking cap.

The fella in the Lexus throws in some loose change. The driver of the Altima donates a buck.

Then he raps on my window.

I remove my wallet. Empty. I used all my cash for a tip at a Mexican restaurant.

"I'm sorry, sir," I tell him. "I'm out."

"Hey man," he's saying. "Don't apologize. I should be the one who's sorry, I've never done this kinda thing before. It's frickin' humiliating. God bless."

This bearded man looks just like my late father.

The rain is coming down harder. The light turns green. I want to say more, but the line of vehicles blows by him.

I can't think about anything else after I leave. Maybe because he looked like he hadn't eaten. Maybe because he had those familiar green eyes.

Damn me, for not having cash. Why is it I have plenty of money when it comes to buying fishing rods, new clothes, or beer? But a man needs supper, and all I can say is, "Sorry, pal."

My mama would be proud.

I pull into a gas station. I ask the cashier where I can find an ATM. She shrugs. So I ask how I can get cash off my card. She says she can't help me, their machine is broken.

I leave. I ride to the nearest supermarket. I can't see taillights ahead because of the rain. The long walk from my truck is like swimming across the Mississippi.

"Credit or debit?" the cashier asks.

"Debit," says Mister Soaked Britches.

I get forty bucks. The girl behind the counter tells me to "Have a nice day," with as much sincerity as it would take her to scratch her hindparts.

I drive back to the stoplight where I see the homeless man. He's sitting on the curb, smoking. I honk.

He pokes his head inside my window and says, "You again?"

He smells like whiskey and Camels.

I hand him money.

He thanks me, but won't take it.

He says, "I'm being honest with everyone who gives me handouts, man. I'm not gonna lie, I'm an alcoholic, dude."

Those eyes. He's a dead ringer for the man who taught me to fish.

I insist. So he takes the money.

"Just want you to know," he goes on. "I'm not a bad man. My name's Bill. I'm just like you."

We shook hands.

"I'm really trying to get my life together, man. But, well, here I am."

Friend, I don't care who you are or why you are here. Alcoholics need supper just like anyone else.

Dear God, look after Bill.

LAND OF COTTON

I don't know his real name, but his friends call him Bubba. He has skin darker than walnut, and a white fuzzy beard.

I met him once. He raises bluetick hounds on a farm with his son, selling them to gun-dog lovers everywhere.

In the short time we talked, he told me about marching from Selma to Montgomery as a young man. About Doctor King. About getting arrested during the riots.

Nice man.

Then, there's the elderly woman I met outside Opp who raised sixteen kids. Sixteen. Her hair, still as red as copper.

She lived in a twelve-by-twelve shed her son made into an apartment—complete with flat-screen television and AC.

Her son told me, "In a big family, we used'a compete for Mama's attention. Man, I feel so lucky she lives with me."

Don—an old man who weighs a buck ten. Maybe less. He runs a mechanic shop out of a barn in North Florida. Auto collectors come from all over for him to work on rare vehicles.

"Started this business after I got outta prison," he said. "Was in the pen four years."

I asked why they locked him up.

"Mary Jane," he answered.

Lydia. She is Birmingham's June Cleaver—Scarlett O'Hara accent. Her nineteen-year-old daughter contracted a rare disease while on a mission trip in Africa. She died suddenly.

Lydia is flying out this week to retrieve her daughter's body.

"When you have a daughter," she said. "You imagine your little girl will get married some day. You never think this will happen."

John, from North Georgia. He's a man who shoots dove and deer on weekends. Once, he was a high-powered attorney. Today, he works part time at Home Depot so he has time to care for his wife with MS.

John said, "Having so much time with my wife is a privilege. Mostly, we watch a lotta Netflix."

Why am I telling you this? Because.

I overhead someone in a restaurant today. Three someones. Men in business suits, sitting in the booth behind me. One made a derogatory remark about Southerners.

I won't tell you what he said because this world has enough foul remarks.

No sooner had he said it, than his pal pointed at a heavyset fella wearing a camouflage hat.

"Look guys," he whispered. "There's Johnny redneck now."

They had a nice laugh.

Look, I'm not upset—even if this fella does have his head shoved halfway up his molasses jar. But it hurts my feelings. Because he's got this place all wrong. He's got everything wrong.

I guess that's why I'm writing this. Because I wish he could meet a few folks that make up a place where old times are not forgotten.

Starting with Bubba.

HOW PRIDE KILLED MY DADDY

We had a bench by our pond. A pine-log bench. It sat near the edge of the water. Daddy called it the Thinking Bench. I remember the day he built it—using only a sharp axe and cuss words.

It's funny, how I can remember things like benches, but not the last words he ever said to me.

Weeds grew around his bench. He trimmed the grass using a jack knife. Cody, his Lab, would sit beside him.

One December morning, when the weather was unusually cold, I found him there. He'd been sitting all night. He wasn't moving. Eyes open. There was a thin layer of frost on his back and shoulders. His red hair stiff from the cold.

Mama ran outside with a blanket. He didn't want it.

"You could'a froze to death," she said. "You need serious help."

"Help doing what?" he'd say with vinegar in his voice.

He didn't trust shrinks. Besides, nobody seemed to know what professional help was. Fewer understood depression. Back then, these were modern ideas used by folks who ate snails at dinner parties.

Daddy was the kind who made log benches. The kind who liked to sit.

Toward the end of his life, you could find him sitting in his workshop, shirtless. Lights off. No music. Staring.

Or: on the hood of his truck, parked on fifty acres. Leaning against his windshield. Or: in the corner of the barn, on the floor, knees pulled to his chest. Eyes pink and wet.

"What's wrong, Daddy?" I'd ask.

He'd wipe his face. "I don't know, dammit."

"Will he be okay?" I'd ask Mama.

"I don't think so," she'd say, giving honest answers—she was through pretending. "He needs help."

The day of his funeral, people with phony grins lined up to shake my hand, saying things like, "Your daddy was just sick..."

I heard that a million and three times. It offended me. These people hardly knew the man they were diagnosing. And it offended me even more that they were right.

He was sick. He quit his life with his hunting rifle. Only someone sick could do that.

Anyway, I'm not sad—and I don't mean to make you sad. You deserve to be happy. In fact, that's why I'm writing this.

I don't know whether you cry when nobody's watching. I don't know if you get so sad you can't do anything but sit. Or if you have a young son who thinks your log benches are the best things since sliced tomatoes.

If you do, I want to tell you something:

Swallow your damned pride before it kills you. And get help.

FLORIDATOWN TEACHER

Pace, Florida—today, the town is suburbia, but once it was Small Floridatown, USA. Think: men in camouflage, women in pearls, millworkers.

Schoolteachers.

Seventeen-year-old Jena was a good student. She had more ambition than her one-horse rural world could hold.

"In my first literature class assignment," says Jena. "I wrote that I wanted to move far, far away from home and be a pediatrician."

But good teachers have X-ray vision. They know which students will be pediatricians, lawyers, pipefitters, and which little hellcat wrote the F-word on the boy's restroom wall.

When Jena's teacher handed back her essay, it read:

"Dear Jena, I don't think you're supposed to be a doctor. I think you're supposed to be a teacher."

What nerve. But then, teachers are like that.

After high school, Jena attended the University of Florida.

"We exchanged a lot of emails once I left her classroom," says Jena. "She really cared."

But she was more than caring. The woman was pure love.

Four years and fifteen million essays later, Jena graduated. And just like her teacher predicted, she became an educator.

Jena made the five-hour drive back to Pace to visit the old classroom.

It was a school day. Class was in session. Jena walked the halls to room 221. She pressed her ear to the door. A familiar voice with a thick drawl was reading aloud to the class.

Jena slipped into a seat on the back row to listen. When class was over, she stood before the teacher's desk like old times.

Before she could say anything, her teacher handed her a binder.

"What's this?"

"I made it for you," her teacher said.

Jena thumbed through it, starting with the first page. Every letter and email they'd ever exchanged.

And on the last page: an essay written by a restless seventeen-year-old who once wanted to "move far, far away."

When Jena read it, Niagara Falls.

Anyway, I'm getting ahead of myself.

This story isn't about Jena at all. Neither is it about the difference she's made as a teacher. Nor about the myriads she's affected as a well-loved principal.

It's about a woman in Pace, who teaches AP Literature in room 221. A lady who has the power to change lives and does it free of charge.

I asked Jena if there was anything else she wanted to say about her teacher.

"Hmm," she said. "Well, her favorite flower's the tulip, it reminds her that God hasn't forgotten about her."

I hope someone gives that woman fifty-acres of tulips.

Because nobody could forget Mrs. Bell.

POCKET CHRISTMAS

Christmas afternoon. I drove my truck down a familiar gravel road. It's a road I can see in my sleep. I hadn't made that drive in many years.

I pulled over on a small bridge, flipped on my hazards. I crawled underneath the bridge. It was muddy. Creek water flooded my boots. I dug with a hand shovel.

This was ridiculous.

My childhood Christmases were simple. Each member of my family received three gifts—which was a rule of Daddy's. Growing up poor changes a man.

One gift was practical. Blue jeans, slacks, or, God forbid, underpants. The other two were fun.

One year I got an LP record,—"Stardust," by Willie Nelson—a cap gun, and khakis.

Mama opened her gift. It was a booklet I'd made from colored paper, entitled: "Mama's Coupons." Inside were various pencil-written discounts. "One free kitchen sweeping," or, "Seventy-percent off hugs," and my personal favorite, "Free ice cream supper."

She never cashed in on the last one.

Daddy's gift was was a bathrobe. Mama made it. It was a sweet gesture. Except, of course, my father didn't wear robes. He crawled out of bed fully dressed with boots on.

He slid it over his clothes, anyway.

Our gift-opening took ten minutes, tops. Then, I ate so much at lunch my feet swelled and my ears rang.

After lunch, Daddy asked if I wanted to go for a walk. I'd expected him to say that. Daddy couldn't sit still for more than a few blinks, not even on holidays.

So we walked. We followed the creek. The small water cut through the woods. We marched through the undergrowth until we came to a concrete bridge.

We sat on the railing, legs dangling. I reached into my coat and handed him a wrapped box the size of a butter stick. The gift-tag, covered in my sloppy handwriting.

"To: Daddy," it read.

He made a face. "What's this? Why'd you get me something?"

Because I'm a sentimental little cuss, that's why.

He tore the paper. It was a pocketknife. Remington. Bone handle. I bought it for ten bucks at the hardware store.

He inspected it. His eyes glazed. Then, he reached in his pocket and handed me his own knife. A Case knife. Old. Yellow handle. Double blade.

"Trade ya," he said.

The week he died, the gentleman at the crematorium handed me a paper sack. "Steel won't melt," he informed me. Inside the sack was a pocketknife and a wallet.

I buried two knives beneath the bridge that night.

And one fateful Christmas afternoon, I dug through fifteen years of creek mud and muck to get them back.

I only found one.

But it was the right one.

GIVE ME THE GOOD OLD DAYS

I'm breaking promises I made long ago. Once, I swore I'd never write anything that smelled even faintly like a Gimme-The-Good-Old-Days sort of story. The kind with sentences like, "kids, when I was your age."

I've given up the fight.

Today, I went fishing. It was chilly. A skiff trolled around my beat-up boat.

It was a teenage couple. They were supposed to be fishing. Instead, they argued loud enough to beat the band. Their screaming voices traveled across the water.

Their fight ended with a round of name-calling. The young man called the girl a horrid name beginning with the sixth letter of the alphabet.

She fired back something worse.

After the fight, they spent the next hour playing on cellphones. No talking.

And just like that, my promise went out the window.

The first thing I'd like to say is:

I'd rather cut out my liver with a dull melon-baller than call a lady a name that rhymes with "truck-face." Such an act would be an affront to the woman who raised me.

Second: put your phones away, kids.

A few days ago, it was Christmas. I visited my

buddy's house. After his kids opened gifts, the children hibernated on the sofa. There, they interacted with Apple products, thumb-tapping, for three hours.

Three.

I asked if anyone wanted to play cards. They looked at me like I had lobsters crawling out my pants. Thus, I played solitaire.

That's too bad. Cards were a big deal during my childhood. I remember playing poker on the kitchen table with uncles who kept spitting into paper cups.

Back then, we had no smartphones. We had big stupid ones with cranks and four-digit phone numbers. The smartest device in our household was Mama—who could expound on anything from navigating to the interstate, to curing black lung using baking soda.

So, even though I swore I'd never say this: I miss the days before intelligent devices.

I miss a time when instant communication among peers meant riding bikes. When children had energy to play all day, and still would.

Don't misunderstand me. I don't want to go back in time—that would mean pimples and school dances. And I don't hate technology, either. I'm a big fan of the calculator.

What I wish is that we had a few more simple things. I wish more people knew that love can be built using nothing but words and smiles. That calling someone names is a lot like murder.

I wish the kids in the boat beside me would tell each other how beautiful the other one is and mean it.

But above all, I wish they'd turn off their phones.

'BACCA PICKERS

"My mother's wedding ring was aluminum," she says, showing me a ring.

The gray band is not a perfect circle, the metal is too cheap to hold its shape.

"I wish I had more pictures of Mother when she was a kid," she goes on. "They say she was a knockout."

A knockout and a tobacco picker. She and her sisters picked 'bacca during harvest seasons near Butler County. They'd been doing it since childhood.

They worked long hours, earned pennies, lived in bunk-cabins, and made new friends. Think: summer camp for poor folks.

By age seventeen, she was still picking each season. On weekends, she and her girlfriends hiked into the woods with the other workers. They lit bonfires, laughed. Some folks brought instruments and jelly-jars. Others wore Sunday shoes.

There she met a skinny boy. He caught her eye. There was something about him. He asked her to dance. She said yes.

It didn't take long to know him—they both worked in the drying barn. She'd string blanket-sized leaves onto pine rods. He'd climb the rafters, hanging them.

He was her first boy. For two summers they kissed.

And two summers they picked side by side. When he asked her to marry, her answer was no surprise.

Then, the worst.

Only one day before their courthouse wedding, she and her sisters went into town to buy a skirt-suit for the ceremony. She walked up a flight of steps, carrying her sister's baby. She slipped.

She dropped the infant on the pavement. The baby was fine, but she wasn't. She busted her neck. They sent her to Tallahassee. Doctors said she might never walk again.

They say he refused to leave her bedside. Not even for food.

After staying motionless for weeks, her temper wore thin. She hollered, told him to leave. She said he deserved a girl in good health, not someone who might need a wheelchair.

He said nothing to her. Then he left. She watched him go and did not call for him. They say she cried.

That evening, while her sister held vigil, a skinny boy came waltzing through the door wearing a ratty suit. He carried a bouquet. He had the preacher with him.

And two cheap rings.

By now, this story practically tells itself. She made a full recovery and later whipped out five kids who all found success in life—except for the youngest, who became a guitar player.

She loved him until her end. He loved her until his.

"This ring was Daddy's," her daughter says sliding it on her own finger. "I wish I had both rings, for my kids."

But that will never happen.

Because her mother is still wearing hers.

HOME OF THE THROWED ROLLS

Foley, Alabama—I'm sitting in Lambert's restaurant. This is the "home of throwed rolls." Servers stroll the dining rooms, tossing yeast rolls at customers like four-seam fastballs.

A waiter lobs one at me. It hits me square in the teeth. He laughs. So does my wife.

It leaves a mark.

Our waitress brings our plates. Chicken-fried steak, collards, fried potatoes. She wishes me a happy New Year and asks, "Have you had a good twenty-sixteen?"

You bet your suspenders I have.

While I haven't done anything noteworthy this year, I did get rid of our rusted 1974 mobile home. That was a biggie.

It got hauled to the county dump by a team of highly specialized ambulatory demolition experts with names like, Delmar, and—I'm not making this up—Willie Joe Mavis.

When the lovable single-wide left our property, it bore a yellow banner, reading, "oversized load."

Willie played "Taps" on the bugle.

Another 2016 highpoint: I kept a New Year's resolution. A little over three hundred days ago, I resolved before King and country to go fishing every weekday at 2 P.M.—even if only for ten minutes—and if need be, to include beer.

It wasn't always easy, but the Lord provides.

The truth is, this has been the best year of my life. And I'm not just saying that.

Let me tell you about Randy.

We grew up together. He was a kindhearted soul who raised four kids on a millworker's salary. He and his wife were salt-of-the earth folks. They ate healthy, abstained from alcohol, sodas, sugar, and barbecue.

He was raised as a foot-washing Baptist and could quote the Old Testament backwards—eyes shut.

I once watched Randy get caught in a fistfight outside a beer-joint. Randy wasn't drinking. He refused to throw a punch and he got beat to a pulp. His soft-spokeness was something to see.

Randy died this year. Doctors never saw it coming. Nobody did. His wife stood on their porch watching an ambulance escort the body of a forty-two-year-old to the county morgue.

Gone.

It rattled me. What's my point?

This: tonight I watched a sunset in a peanut field. Beside me was a woman who once promised she'd grow old with me. She hooked her arm around mine and said, "I'm cold, honey."

So we went to Lambert's.

I'm no fool. I know that nothing lasts forever. One day, she or I will give up breathing, and the other will give up smiling. One day, there will be no peanut fields, no arm-hooking, and no yeast rolls.

Don't let anyone tell you the best is yet to come. We're alive.

It's already here.

DON'T MAKE ME SAY IT

It's too big to write about. But, I'm not going to let that stop me. That's because it's a pretty big thing I'm referring to. The biggest.

Jaden owes his very life to this thing.

Jaden was an abandoned infant born with crack-cocaine in his bloodstream. After his mother's arrest, he was adopted by Claire—sixty-eight-year-old single woman who heard about his situation through a friend.

Claire said, "I know I ain't got forty years to give'im like some young couples, but I'm a good mama, he can have every year I got left."

Consequently, this "big thing" is the same thing that killed Bob Cassidy.

First, it compelled Cassidy to pull over on Highway 10 to change a woman's tire. A car struck him. It killed him on impact.

I know what you're thinking, "What a senseless tragedy." It wasn't senseless. All thanks to this thing we're talking about.

This thing also prompted Betty to adopt three rescue dogs from a kill-shelter. She brought them home and turned them loose on her twenty-acre farm.

"That's when it hit me," she said. "I knew I had enough room for lotsa dogs."

So she drove back and adopted several more. Then a few more. Soon, the shelter started giving them to her.

Folks thought Betty was nuts. But she's not. She only looks that way to people who don't know about this thing —which often makes normal folks look like they're a few bricks short of a load.

Don't get me wrong, this thing isn't always petunias and soap bars. This thing can be hard as nails. Sometimes, it causes the greatest pain you'll ever feel. Even so, it's a pain worth feeling. Don't ask me why. I don't know.

Something I do know:

This stuff is the fabric the universe. It's the only real thing out there. It's what makes average people sparkle, and ugly skies look pretty. It gives purpose to death. It brings mamas and daddies together, and makes memories immortal.

The evening news claims it's difficult to find. They're wrong. It's everywhere, even in that breath you just took. It's in biscuits for crying out loud.

No religion owns it, no government can control it, and it will never be for sale. It's older than you are. It will outlive your children's children's children's children. It will line the pockets of poor folks, and turn hell-raisers into deacons.

It will move mountain ranges, stop divorces, pay your car insurance, deliver your baby, and it saved a wretch like me. I'm going to write about it until they lay me down.

I don't care what you name it.

Jaden calls it love.

NEW YEAR'S EVE

10:40 P.M.—New Year's Eve. Hank Williams is on my radio. My wife is sleeping in the passenger seat. My coonhound is in the backseat.

To bring in the year, we've gone for a drive on county roads that weave along the Choctawhatchee Bay.

There are no cars out. The highway is vacant—except for police cruisers. I've never welcomed in a year like this.

As a boy, my father and I brought in holidays with shotguns. We'd march to the edge of creation and fire twelve gauges at the moon. Then, I'd sip Coca-Cola; he'd sip something clear.

Another year goes by without him.

11:02 P.M.—my tank is on E. I stop at a gas station. The pump card-reader is broken. My wife is still out cold.

I go inside to pay. The clerk is a young girl with purple hair. She wanted to be with her kids tonight, but someone called in with a sinus infection.

I buy a Coca-Cola in a plastic bottle.

I also buy a scratch-off lotto ticket. The last few minutes of the year, I'm feeling lucky. I use my keys to scratch the ticket. I win five bucks. So, I buy another two. I win another dollar.

"Lucky you," the cashier says. "Wish I could buy one, but it's against store policy."

To hell with policy. It's New Year's Eve.

I buy her one.

She swipes a coin from the take-a-penny tray. She scratches. She wins ten bucks. We high-five.

It's only ten bucks, but seeing her win makes my year.

11:28 P.M.—I'm driving. My wife is still sawing pinelogs. I'm riding though the North Florida woods, sipping Coke. Trees grow so high you can't see the moon. It's almost like poetry.

Long ago, my college professor told us to choose a poem to recite in class. Students chose lofty selections from the greats. Whitman, Dickinson, Frost.

I consulted Daddy's Hank Williams songbook. He'd given it to me before he died. He'd wanted to be a guitar player once upon a time, but he was god-awful. He gave the instrument to me.

I recited, "I'm So Lonesome I Could Cry," and made a D.

I wasn't doing it for the teacher.

11:40 P.M.—my Coke is almost empty. I'm parked on the edge of the bay to watch fireworks. My coonhound is looking at me with red eyes. And I'm writing you, just like I do every day.

Listen, I don't remember how I started writing, or why. I have nothing valuable to say, I don't know any big words, and I'm as plain as they come. But I won't lie to you, it has been precious to me. And so have you.

These are my last words of the old year, my first words of the new:

I love you.

Happy New Year.

DO THIS NOT THAT

Girls. The world owes you an apology. The television, the magazines, the news reports, and all mankind. They've done you wrong. And I, for one, am sorry about it.

They're trying to kill you. And once they've finished, they're going after your daughters.

Don't believe me? Just flip on the TV. They say you're not sexy enough. You're overweight. Your swimsuit isn't tiny enough. Your hair should be blonder, darker, straighter, and you need more volume.

Not only that, but you're dowdy. Your lips are too small; hips too big. You've got bags under your eyes, your teeth could be whiter, chest bigger, arms less flabby, midsection tighter.

I'm just warming up.

You need new clothes, new shoes, and it'd be nice if you could find a pair of better-fitting, more expensive jeans. Your skin is old-looking, you need a tan, a firmer hindsection, lose that baby-weight, and wax those forearms.

You talk too much. You don't cook enough. You're not strict enough with your kids. You need regular exercise twice per hour.

You need more school, more credibility, more accredited classes, more professional know-how, management skills, leadership training, certifications, administrative growth.

And for God's sake, get a little confidence.

You drink too much coffee, not enough coconut water. You consume too much butter, not enough palm oil. You don't eat quinoa, pomegranate, kale, bone broth, kombucha, brewer's yeast.

What's wrong with you? Are you trying to kill yourself?

You eat too much bacon, butter, ham, beef, cheese, potatoes, and fried chicken. Clean up your diet. Clean up your potty mouth. And fold that laundry.

Read this book—everyone's reading it. Go see that movie—it's the most important film of our decade. Keep up with current events. Sign your boy up for every sporting team available. Make sure your daughter practices piano.

Hate these people, they deserve it. Don't talk to her, she's got a bad reputation. Never give handouts to the homeless—you don't know how they'll spend it. Trust no one. Question everything.

Don't believe in God. Instead, tell people you're spiritual.

You're too young. You're too old. You're too tall, too short, too uneducated, too talkative, too shy, too serious, too silly, too stupid, too weak, too ugly, too narrow-minded, too outside-the-box, too unmotivated.

They are telling you who you are and what you should be doing. You've seen them in every checkout-aisle magazine, internet ad, and underwear commercial. There's no way you could miss them, they're practically shouting at you from each corner of the room.

Well, I hope you're still listening, girls. Because now it's my turn to say something.

They're liars. Every damn one. And they owe you an apology.

Because there is no such thing as imperfection.

THE WORLD AIN'T ALL BAD

Freeport, Florida—my friend found a car stuck in a muddy ditch on a secluded road. It had just rained. The ground was soft. The thing was buried up to the bumpers.

It was full of Mexican women who didn't speak English. My pal asked if they needed help—he happens to speak fluent hand-gestures.

All they could say was, "Please, yessir, thank you."

They were a cleaning crew. Each of them had taken turns digging around the tires. Their uniforms were covered in mud. They had wet eyes.

My buddy strapped the vehicle to his hitch. It wouldn't budge. He tried everything. No luck. So, he called some friends with trucks who lived nearby.

I was one such friend.

Three of our trucks lined up, side by side. We strung tow ropes to the vehicle, then hit the gas at the same time. Seven strangers, eight shovels, two Chevies, one Ford, and many years later...

My pal married one of those girls.

Quincy, Florida—Walmart. An elderly woman in the checkout aisle. She didn't look good. She walked with a bent back, hunched shoulders, and carried a cane.

A manager helped her unload the cart. Then he paid

her bill. A girl waiting in line videoed the whole thing on her cellphone.

The manager said to the girl, "Please turn off your camera, this doesn't belong on Facebook. Show some respect, please."

She put the camera away.

Then wrote me a letter about it.

Jonesboro, Georgia—he used to be a preacher. A good one. Then he had a wreck. It damaged his back. He got hooked on painkillers and whiskey.

The church fired him. He lost his wife, kids, and ambition. Which made him drink more.

One day, the church janitor showed up on his doorstep. He treated the former pastor to breakfast. Together, they ate too much bacon, drank too much coffee, and laughed too much.

He showed up again the next morning. And the next. It became routine. Soon, they were hunting together, going on fishing trips.

The preacher finally asked, "Why didn't you write me off, like everyone else?"

The man showed him a sobriety token.

Anyway, I feel I owe it to you to admit: I don't know much about life—I have the lack of training to prove it.

Even so, I'm a person who believes in something. In miracles. Small ones I've seen with my own eyes. In people. In things that terrify the sapsuckers who write the nightly news—folks who earn livings reporting on the worst mankind has to offer.

Well, I think life is a lot more than a string of bad headlines. If you don't believe me...

You ought to attend a Mexican wedding.

DEAR SEAN

DEAR SEAN:
A friend of mine introduced me to your writing. I've only read a little, but as a retired copy editor, and author of two books, I think you could use some work.

You write about life. Well, I was married twenty-four years... My husband had an affair with a much younger woman. I know a little about the pain of life.

I've never lived on my own before, I'm in my late-fifties, I've raised two kids, and I'm all alone this year.

Your brand of goody-goody writing represents what's wrong with this country. I'm sorry to be so blunt, your intentions are probably pure, but you're still too ostensibly young to know how hard life is, honey. People don't need more lovey-dovey ignorance crap. Sometimes it's healthy to embrace anger.

Sincerely,
JUST BEING REAL

DEAR REAL:
I've always wanted to do the Dear Abby thing, so thanks for signing your letter that way. Also: I won't lie, I had to look up "ostensibly" in the dictionary.

I appreciate your honesty. Allow me to return the favor.

You're right about me. I don't know how hard life is. My father shot himself with a rifle the day he got out of jail. My mother locked herself in her room and cried for years. My family eroded. I was twelve.

I don't want to talk much about it. It's ostensibly difficult.

I hope I used that word right.

What I can tell you is that we lived on a farm. The day Daddy passed, adult-chores fell to adolescent-me. So did the laundry. I was angry. Not just with my father, but with my peers, for having easy lives.

Eventually, we lost the farm. We lost lots of things—that's what happens to poor folks.

Mama cleaned condos, I swung hammers. We delivered newspapers, laid sod, painted houses. We got good at hocking things. Once, I even took a job digging a drainage ditch with a Venezuelan man named Salvador. I slept in his van for three days.

It was actually a nice van—with a kitchenette.

The things you'll do for rent.

So you're right. I don't know what it's like to have a husband walk out. In fact, I don't know half the things you do. I've never claimed to be the sharpest hammer in the bag.

Here's what I know:

I know life comes bundled in ugly wrapping paper. I'm sorry, that's just how it is, ma'am. We can either get angry—God knows we deserve that much. Or we can tear open the hideous package and see the gift inside.

I guess what I really mean to say is: I'm sorry he hurt you. In fact, it breaks my damn heart, darling.

Ostensibly yours,
Sean Dietrich

GRANDMAMA OF THE YEAR

I have a bad ankle. I don't know what I did to it, but it's been nagging me for months. I visited the doctor. He looked like a twelve-year-old.

He frowned at me, then said—and I quote: "Sucks getting old, doesn't it?"

I paid a lot of money to hear Junior say that.

The nurse fitted me with an ankle brace. She was elderly. Skinny. Everything she said sounded like sorghum. In the short time she helped me, we made friends.

There's a tattoo on her hand. Two interlocking hearts. I asked about it—you don't see many tattoos on someone who looks like Granny.

"My daughter made me get this," she said. "We got matching ones when she graduated."

I did the math. This woman seemed awfully long in the tooth to have a child so young.

She must've known I was confused because she laughed. "She's actually my granddaughter."

Well, as it happens, her granddaughter is her daughter. When the child was a one-year-old, her mother shot herself. Nobody knew who the father was.

"It was traumatic," she said. "When we found her, she was laying on her mama's body, asleep."

She speaks without flinching.

She adopted her granddaughter. And since babies are expensive, her husband went back to work. But it was a struggling economy. There wasn't much work.

They agreed she'd come out of retirement and go back to nursing.

Her certifications had expired, the medical world had advanced. They told her she'd have to complete nearly as much school as entry-level students.

"Lord," she said. "Didn't think I'd been gone THAT long. But things had changed. When I's in school, we didn't have Google."

Her husband wasn't sure if it was a good idea. Neither was she. Hard studying, odd hours, clinical shifts.

She enrolled anyway.

As it happened, the refresher courses weren't bad. Not for her. She had more experience than some of her professors.

"I studied eight hours a day, six days a week, just to keep up with the teeny-boppers. I kept telling myself, 'You can do anything for that baby, she deserves your best,' you know?"

Yeah.

That seems like a lifetime ago, she explains. Her granddaughter just finished college. There's no need for this woman to work ER shifts anymore, so she claims she's about to retire.

I asked if I could write about her.

"Me?" she says. "What for? I'm just a little old woman."

Ma'am, you might very well be old.

You aren't little.

REAL MOTHERS

I used two words and made a fat mistake. I guess that's progress. Usually, it only takes me one word.

Anyway, I wrote about an adopted girl. I referred to her mother as an "adoptive mother."

Poor choice of words. Mothers who adopt are REAL mothers. Those who give children up for adoption are "birth-mothers."

Adoptive mothers don't exist.

Sometimes I have the IQ of a room-temperature Budweiser.

That day, I received forty-two messages from parents of adopted children, and step-parents. They all had adoption stories. These were kindhearted letters from people with so much sweetness they make pound cake look bland.

I read each message aloud to my wife. It took me an afternoon to read through them—it was one of the finest afternoons I've had in a while.

Here's why:

One woman wrote: "I was working as a waitress. This girl who washed dishes was pregnant and told me in passing that she was going to abort her baby because her boyfriend had landed in jail...

"I didn't sleep all night. The next day I just went right

up to her, my hands were trembling, and asked if she'd let me and my boyfriend adopt.

"It's been a long road, but the bottom line is, my son is my pride and joy. I've never looked back. I just wanted you to know that I fully consider myself his real mother."

As you should, ma'am.

Another friend writes: "When I heard I couldn't have kids it made me feel like I was a broken washing machine or something.

"The day we first held our baby girl my husband said I smiled so big... He says I looked like an unused coloring book who was finally getting colored in—I don't know if that makes sense."

It does.

Someone else: "My son was born in a bad part of town... People were doing meth, trading drugs for sex. Later, we found out his birth-mother was wasn't only an addict, she was a kind of local prostitute.

"My son had a distended belly from not eating proper, and he was close to slipping into a coma.

"Someone dropped him off at the hospital anonymously. We got him through our pastor... I used to stay awake praying over him while he slept. We were so relieved when we found out he didn't have AIDS.

"You should see how healthy he is today. He's not even the same kid."

There's a selfish hatred running loose in the streets. I don't know what you call it, but it's everywhere. And it's gutting families from the inside out. Even so, I'm not afraid of it.

Not anymore.

You shouldn't be either. Because there are people who are fighting against it and winning.

They're called real mothers.

I'm sorry I ever called them anything else.

HARD BISCUITS

She was shouting in a general store, hollering until her voice broke.

And back in those days, women didn't holler.

It was a small store; a tiny town. It was the kind of market where the cashiers knew your name—and asked about your mama.

The screaming lady waved her finger at a man wearing a necktie. She was dressed in rags. She had wiry auburn hair, sad eyes, rough hands, three kids—filthy ones.

The owner asked the woman to lower her voice.

But the woman would not. She could not. This was a Depression, the only thing she had left was a voice. Her children hadn't eaten in two days. Her eldest boy was losing hair in clumps.

The store owner had no charity. He was new in town. He didn't know her from Adam, nor did he care for women who shouted.

She told him how the previous store owner let the family charge groceries on an account. On the first of every month, she put money toward the bill—though it was never enough.

He wouldn't hear her.

She screamed, telling him she had no husband. She

told him how she took in wash for a pittance. She pleaded for beans, salt pork, or even a few tins of hard biscuits.

The new shop owner was fresh out of pity, a business man. The only things he knew about this woman were in his logbook.

He removed the food from her basket by force. The kids wailed. She slapped him. He kicked her out and warned her not to come back until she settled her debt. Then he called the sheriff.

She left in tears.

For supper that evening: water and hollow tummies. The oldest boy later recounted that he was so hungry he felt drunk. Sometimes he laughed for no reason. Then cried.

The next morning, the family awoke to loud noises on the porch. She walked downstairs and flung open the door.

People.

They stood on her doorstep with caged chickens, sacks of flour, pinto beans, rice, butter, milk, and hams. They say all she could do was blink.

Folks took turns embracing her. The sheriff himself offered her a tin biscuit-box filled with money.

He explained how several neighbors had taken up a collection. How even he himself had knocked on doors, asking for food and money. In the end, they didn't raise much, but it was enough to pay a grocery debt.

She told the people, "I don't want no damned charity," because that's what poor folks say.

He told her, "We love you," because that's what Methodists say.

She accepted the box.

And years later, Grandaddy gave the box to me.

NAME CALLING

I wasn't going to write this. But I did anyway.

Yesterday, I got accused of being a Christian. It was an odd insult. He said the word hatefully.

I didn't answer.

So he said it again.

I paid my tab and walked outside to get some air.

The first thing you should know is that I had it coming. Earlier that evening, I'd asked the perfect stranger not to shout the F-word at the restaurant TV. He was watching a game. I don't even know which one.

My pal's six-year-old daughter was in a nearby booth. "Daddy," she said. "Is the F-word really Jesus' middle name?"

So I asked the man if he'd keep it down.

"Who the hell're you?" he said, standing. He towered over me by at least fifty thousand nautical miles. "You some mother #%*!ing Christian?"

It surprised me.

I've never been called that before. If he'd truly wanted me to wound me, he went about it all wrong.

This is the deep South. If you want to get a man riled, you call him a "no good sumbitch," then strike a beer bottle briskly against an unforgiving surface.

A Christian.

I won't lie. I've spent a lot of time in church. Religion was in my drinking water. I've even attended services where snakes were handled. My cousin held one with both hands and said he felt the power of the Almighty vibrate his bones.

He sells used cars today.

Anyway, this fella wasn't just insulting me. He was referring to my heritage. The peanut-fields, the sod cabins, summer revivals, and clapboard houses of my ancestry.

The word "Christian" was engraved on my grandaddy's dogtag. And when the bullet struck him, he said the medics hollered his rank and denomination.

This word represents the best memories of my childhood. Sunday school with white-haired ladies who taught us to love fellow human beings—whether red, yellow, black, or white. Gay, lesbian, Muslim, Jew, Latino, left-wing, right-wing, or short thigh.

The word is also potlucks on the green, old-fashioned song services, women who make Nobel-Prize-winning fried chicken.

It's who I talk to when I'm alone. It's hymns I know by heart. It's my childhood pastor who once told me, "I'm sorry, son, your father's gone."

It was in my wedding.

It was with me when I sat in UAB's waiting room, red-eyed and puffy-faced, waiting on results from my wife's biopsy.

It's Granny—who read a beat-up Bible each morning. It's Mama, who still does the same.

Don't misunderstand me, please. I really don't have that much faith. But then, I understand it doesn't take much.

A Christian.

Yes, by God, I guess I am.

MOTHER MARY

My mother-in-law fell yesterday. She stumbled in the garage. It was bad. She smacked her face on the pavement. She busted her glasses. And her nose. When I found her she was bleeding.

"We're going to the ER," I said.

"I feel lightheaded," remarked the white-haired Scarlett O'Hara.

"Yes, ma'am. Here, take my arm."

"Wait, I need to brush my teeth before we go."

"But you're bleeding all over."

"These shoes don't match my belt, get my blue shoes from the closet, the sling-back heels."

"But..."

"...And my lipstick, it's in my purse. I need my pearls."

Meet Mother Mary.

I've called her that ever since our first supper together. That was a long time ago. I remember the meal: rump roast, served with enough trimmings to make the table buckle.

For desert, we had pear salad—a half-pear topped with mayonnaise, shredded cheese, and a cherry. I ate every bite. but you should know: I'd rather lick a possum than eat pear salad.

I nearly choked.

Even so, that night Mary and I discovered we liked each other. She told me to call her Mother Mary. It's all I've ever called her.

Before she was my mother-in-law, I visited once to take her daughter on a movie-date. Her husband answered the door with a twelve-gauge.

"Jamie's upstairs," he said. "Her mama and I are on the pier, fishing."

Her daddy led me to the dock where Mother Mary was working a rod and reel. She started screaming, "I got one!"

Without saying a word, my wife's daddy aimed the double-barrel at the water. He unloaded two explosions and ten cuss words.

It was a speckled trout the size of a grown man's leg.

That night, we canceled our movie date and ate with my wife's parents. Fried fish, hushpuppies, French fries, okra, and anything else her daddy could stuff into a deep-fryer.

I'm hard pressed to remember having a better time. And if I didn't know better, I would've sworn these three people cared about me.

Then Mother Mary brought out pear salad.

Anyway, after our ER visit today, Mother Mary sat in a recliner with a bandaged face. Her wrist is purple, face swollen. She's tired.

And she is tough.

This Bellville-Avenue Belle grew up in a time of cotton dresses, bare feet, and decency. She has survived a handful of dear friends, thirteen US presidents, and one late husband who fished with firearms.

Mother Mary has one titanium hip, crippling rheumatism, and an accent that sounds like azaleas. She brings Brewton, Alabama into any room she enters. And anyone fortunate enough to hear her say at least three words often ends up smiling.

She can arrange flowers, paint with oils, write thank-yous until dawn, and sing any Hank Williams tune.

The doctors did CAT scans, X-rays, and other tests. The young physician remarked that he'd never seen a patient with cleaner teeth and nicer lipstick.

He didn't even mention her pearls.

"I broke my glasses, falling," she told me, covering her bruised face. "They were expensive."

Glasses are cheap.

There will never be another Mary Finlay Martin.

ROLL TIDE ROLL

Freeport, Florida, 8:39 P.M.—Publix. It's halftime for the National Championship. I'm here to buy a sandwich. I just left a party at my friend's house.

Publix is quiet. I'm tired. I'm hungry. The food at the party was god-awful. My pal tried making Mexican cheese dip that tasted like microwave-melted fertilizer.

So I'm here.

There's a woman ahead of me at the sandwich counter. She has a son sleeping in a stroller. He's no baby. In fact, he's not even a small kid, he looks like a fifth-grader.

She's wearing a "Roll Tide" sweatshirt.

And this makes us best friends.

So, we chat football.

While the young man at the counter makes her sandwich, she talks. She tells me she's recently moved back to town. She was raised here, but moved away when she got married.

I asked what brought her back.

"My divorce," she said. "I'm starting over."

Then, we're interrupted by her son.

No sooner does he open his eyes than he's screaming loud enough to affect the climate. He flails his arms. Cries. Kicks. She tries to hush him.

He won't have it.

He throws a plastic toy at her. It hits her square in the face. Hard.

She doesn't react. She only looks at me and says, "He didn't mean that, it's just past his bedtime."

Yeah.

She picks the kid up, holding him like a newborn. The boy is almost as tall as she is. His legs are limp.

Once her sandwiches are made and wrapped, her boy has calmed. She places him back in the stroller. She thanks the man behind the counter.

Then she looks at me. "I know this is weird, but would you mind watching my son while I go to the bathroom? He's finally relaxed, I don't wanna disturb him."

Absolutely, ma'am.

She walks toward the restrooms with her hands over her face.

She's only gone a few minutes. When she gets back, her cheeks are wet, her eyes are bloodshot. And I sincerely doubt she did anything in the restroom but cry.

"Thanks," she says, sniffing. "Sorry about my son."

"Don't be."

"Roll tide," she says. "I hope we win."

And she's gone.

Dear God, I know you're busy. I know you've got folks tugging on your apron from all over the world. I don't know what's going on with that child. But if you have a moment...

Bless the hell out of that woman.

PACE, FLORIDA

I'm watching the sun rise over Interstate 10. It's magnificent. My wife and I ride two hours until we land in Pace, Florida.

The high-school parking lot is full. The school is plain-looking, with Old Glory flying in front. The small campus sits across the road from a cotton field.

In the parking space beside me sits an old truck with Browning stickers on the back. Muddy tires.

This is Small-Town USA.

Miss Carrie gives us the dime tour. The school halls are lined with framed photos of seniors dating back to the Nixon administration. Each portrait is a history lesson in the evolution of bad American hairstyles.

"Our school's special," Miss Carrie says. "Our staff has tried really hard to make it this special."

She leads us into the yearbook room. There's a buffet loaded with biscuits, grits, and bacon.

Special.

My wife and I fix plates and meet the faculty. These are real folks—the sort with accents like your mama's Wednesday night Bible study group. Some teachers have been here forty years. Other are wet behind the ears. There's something different about this lot.

They believe in this cinderblock building.

"You're not gonna find many schools like us anymore," says one woman. "We're old-fashioned."

Miss Carrie shows me a plaque with student names. "I want you to see our exceptional students."

Exceptional. But not because of GPA's. These are students who overcome adversity, who help others. The kinds of qualities Pace thinks are important.

She taps the plaque. "This girl had a cognitive disorder, she had to work twice as hard as other kids. We're all really proud'a her. She deserves to be honored."

This must be heaven.

So, why am I telling you about an ordinary high school, sitting behind a plow field? You already know why. Because this is the American South. And it's precious.

Because this is a school with a hunting-fishing club that prints its own camouflage. Where teachers still call you "sweetie"—even when you're in hot water. Where your principal knows your daddy personally, and your athletic director is the kind of moral gentleman you hope God might one day make you into.

This is a place where violence only happens on Friday-night fields. Where any child who hurts has real-life angels who will shake the earth for their cause.

"The way we see it," says one woman. "We're not just teachers, we're the last line of defense. Our most important job is love. That's how we better this world. That's how we better America."

When breakfast is over, I ask a teacher what the school mascot is. He shows me a red and blue logo on his shirt.

"We're the Patriots," he says.

Yes you are.

You certainly are.

ALABAMA LOSER

She's had a hard life. I can tell. Her skin is rough, she's got wiry brown hair, and if I'm not mistaken, false teeth.

She's on class break, standing on the sidewalk. She offers me a smoke. I decline.

The closest I've ever come to being a smoker was sitting with my grandaddy while he lit his pipe.

I ask her why she's here.

She flicks her lighter and tells me, "Because I'm a flunky."

Her first marriage ended when her husband got hooked on painkillers. One day, she found him unconscious. He almost overdosed. That's when her life changed.

She took her kids and left.

"I tried to find a good job," she says. "But there ain't good jobs out there for flunky losers, that's something I learned real fast."

The first thing you should know: she's no flunky. In fact, she's the opposite. I don't know her, but I know her sort. She descends from a long line of South Alabamians who work like mutts.

"Two days after I left him," she says. "I signed up to take GED prep classes."

School was hard. Hours were late. She was no spring chicken, and working a day-job makes a body tired. To make matters worse, she had a bad instructor.

"He was a jerk," she remarks. "He talked too fast, and didn't care if we understood things."

So, she took charge. She self-taught. Once she'd learned the material, she wandered from desk to desk, helping others diagram sentences, memorize multiplication, and solve for X.

Flunkies.

"Listen," she says "That test is tough, took eight hours to finish."

Eight.

"Had to break mine up into two days. I thought for sure I'd failed. I flat-out cried when they gave me my graduation slip."

Her eyes glaze.

So do mine. All that smoke.

"I didn't think paper would matter so much," she says. "But it was like, I mean, when you grow up thinking you're dumb, suddenly they say you ain't…"

So, she began taking classes at the community college. It was a long road. Sometimes, she found herself hustling two jobs just to afford daycare and groceries.

That was a long time ago.

She's passing middle age now. But here she is, still at school in the dark. Smoking on break. And she still tells this story to anyone who listens.

I ask what she does for a living.

"Me? Guess you could say I tell people they ain't stupid, no matter how they been raised."

That's the long version of her job description.

Her students just call her the GED instructor.

ANOTHER SMALL TOWN

Calhoun County, Florida—a small world bordered by the mighty Apalachicola. A rural community, forty minutes south of the Georgia line. A place where you can get live crickets at supermarkets. Where you can still buy plug tobacco.

It's a progressive area.

Here, for instance, they observe Goat Day—a holiday honoring goat-milking, banjos, hell-fire preaching, and greased pig chases.

It bears mention: I've chased a greased pig once—at a Baptist fair. I broke two ribs.

So welcome to Blountstown. It's more than a small town. It's Tonya Lawrence's life. She grew up in these schools, played softball on this dirt, shopped at The Pig, birthed Calhoun-County babies.

One day, she went to the doctor for a routine visit. The doctor ordered lab work. The results were a punch to the face. Her kidneys were shutting down.

Tonya says, "It was devastating, I always considered myself a strong person, but once I started dialysis..."

Yeah.

Seven nights a week, she hooked to a machine, watching her strength run through little tubes.

Her condition isn't just the kind that kills. It's the sort

that ruins your life first.

And there's a problem: kidney-donor lists are more exclusive than US congressional barbecues. It takes a long time to locate an organ. Best case scenario: seven to fourteen years.

Tonya's children will be filing for AARP by then.

Still, this is Old Florida, a place where everybody knows everybody. Where the school principal graduated with your daddy's fishing-buddy's cousin. Where gossip flies across Facebook faster than a greased hog.

Tonya's friends put the word out for donors.

But sadly, this isn't a fairytale. And drumming up vital organs isn't as easy as holding canned-food drives at the sheriff's station. Tonya waited.

In the meantime, she's received affection. Lots of it.

She's been fielding billions of phone calls, responding to texts, tapping out Facebook thank-yous. And I'm willing to bet she received enough gift baskets to compromise her porch's structural stability.

These few years have been hell. But Tonya's not breaking. She tells me her only option is trusting.

Thus, while the rest of the world points cameras at politicians and half-naked celebrities—the heroes which journalists think you should give a damn about—Tonya sits connected to a machine. Praying.

I asked Tonya if I could write about her.

"Me?" she says. "Sure, but can you give me a copy? For a keepsake?"

You bet. And if it's okay, I'd like to drop it off Friday, with some poundcake my wife made.

"Sorry," she says. "Friday won't work, I'm gonna be busy."

Busy. I guess so. This morning, the school principal is giving Tonya one of her kidneys.

Say what you will about small towns.

They own the patent on love.

CAT PEOPLE

Rascal's old. Too old to purr, she sleeps all day, she can't jump anymore. She's twenty years old.

Her back legs quit working months ago—arthritis. And she only eats soft food.

She came into this marriage as Jamie's illegitimate feline. Back then, Rascal was piss and vinegar, wrapped in fur, with a preference for squatting on expensive items.

I don't mind telling you: she used to hate me.

As a young cat, she'd glare at me like Rosemary's Baby. Once, she hid beneath our mattress to avoid a veterinary visit. I tried to remove her; she tried to sever a major artery.

Another time: she vomited in my dress-shoes. And once, on Christmas Eve night, she deposited a holiday miracle on my pillow.

But that's ancient history.

I'm not sure when it happened, but we fell in love. She quit despising me and started waiting in our windowsill for me to arrive home from work.

I even took her fishing once. I gave her a few baitfish. She tortured them, then licked their guts clean.

During football games, she'd sit on our coffee table —beside my beer—watching TV. So help me, the cat watched television.

When I'd holler, "C'mon, dammit!" at Alabama's offense, she'd flick her tail.

And she's a daddy's girl. While I write stories, she sleeps on my desk, between my typewriter and computer. Or in my lap.

I went to pet her last night. A clump of twenty-year-old hair came off in my hand. Her skin is paper. She's been losing weight. Her bones are porcelain

God.

Time is running away. I've changed a lot in twenty years. You wouldn't even recognize the person I used to be, either.

I used to be stupid, impulsive, short-sighted. Long ago, I skipped a college English final to go on a fishing trip. I earned an F.

What was I thinking?

Some days, I look in the mirror and wonder at the new lines on my face.

Today we wrapped Rascal in a blanket and took her to the vet. She laid in my wife's arms while she whispered, "You're a good girl."

And I felt my eyes get wet.

The doc came in with a syringe full of pink stuff.

"Ssssshh, Rascal," said my wife, sobbing.

God decided not to give us kids. We're average individuals whose children come from the local pound.

My offspring are the kind that use litter boxes, or bury bones in the backyard. But they're part of me. I feed them. Pray for them. They ride shotgun. They go fishing.

They even sit on my lap while I write.

At least they used to.

I'm writing alone tonight.

THE FAMILY THAT CLAIMED ME

Early morning. Belleville Avenue. That's me in the kitchen, eating bacon by the handful, wearing a coat and tie.

I just got engaged. My future in-laws are throwing a brunch. My soon-to-be aunt, Catherine, cooked nearly fifty pounds of bacon for this shindig.

I even bought a new shirt for this brunch. Also: a coat, necktie, and new belt—one without a buckle.

"You can't wear a BELT BUCKLE to an engagement party," proclaimed my future-spouse. "People will think you're a 'neck. You need a DRESS belt."

What could be dressier than a fella waltzing around, sporting a Beechnut buckle the size of a pie-plate?

It would never do.

Earlier that week, my wife carried me to JC Penny's in Andalusia. She selected a skinny belt not fit for stroping a razor. And a fifty-dollar button-down with a shirt-tag reading: "wrinkle-free."

I want my money back.

The doorbell rings. Folks in their Sunday best begin to arrive. I've never met these people before, I'm not sure they'll like me. I am sick-to-my-stomach nervous about it because I have about as much sophistication as an empty mayonnaise jar.

Many guests are elderly. Lots of pastel colors. Strings of pearls. Floral hats.

An old woman hugs me. Then another. Then another.

And I smell like lady's perfume in a matter of milliseconds.

Someone invites me to church. Another invites me drinking. One fella invites me to do both.

Next: my future uncle. He's a small Baptist man, with eyes that shine. He shakes my hand, tells me he loves me.

Then, I meet a fella with a prosthetic arm and a warm face. He hands me a silver dollar and winks. I still have that coin.

I meet ten Flossies, five Roberts, one Mary, two aunt Catherines, a Mary-Catherine, eleven Jims, nine hundred Jameses, the West Boys, a Ben, a Bob, a Bill, a Blake.

And one Bentley.

I meet aunts, cousins, childhood teachers, a pastor with perfect hair. Truck drivers, brick layers, and a beef jerky salesman.

By he end of the day, I'm on the sofa. My wife comes into the room and hands me a small gift-wrapped box. It's heavy.

I unwrap it.

"What's this?" I ask. But I can already tell what it is.

"It was my grandaddy's belt buckle," she says. "I thought you'd like this since you're in my family now."

Family.

As it happens, I've spent a long time not belonging to much family. My daddy was a union man, Mama worked at Chick-Fil-A.

I don't know how, but I lost my confidence along the way. And nobody tells you that once you lose self-confidence you may never get it back.

But then, I also believe in second chances. More than I believe in anything else on this cotton-picking planet.

If you don't…

Then it's time you paid a visit to Brewton, Alabama.

PEOPLE I'VE KNOWN

I knew a man who lived in a tent with his twelve-year-old son. He was plumb crazy. The real kind of crazy. He camped in the woods and wouldn't accept money from anyone.

Sometimes, his son would wander into the church next door during potlucks.

The kid's daddy had a heart attack. The last day we saw the boy, a few of us gave him a Tupperware container full of cash—since we didn't know what else to do. The boy just looked at us. I've never felt so pathetic.

He finally said, "God bless you, guys."

If he's still alive, that child is a man today.

Another fella I knew: he was a rodeo king. We'd drink beer together. I'd ask him about the old days. He'd tell me about the steel pins in his hip, plate in his skull, neck fusion, and spinal surgeries. God, could he rope.

When they diagnosed him with prostate cancer, he retired from the circuit and started working at a hardware store.

Once he told me, "The hardest part about dying is wishing I could'a done a few things different."

Hardly anyone came to his funeral. I sat beside his daughter. They put his ashes in a saddle bag.

His daughter said to me, "I thought more people would'a shown up. God bless you for coming."

My friend Davey and I painted houses. But he wasn't a house-painter. Long ago, he taught music at Auburn University. Symphonic composition. The man had orchestras playing in his brain.

He was bad to drink.

Sometimes, I'd visit his one-room apartment and find him face-down in his vomit. He told me once, "It ain't me who drinks, it's my demons. I just can't kill them."

He was purple when the paramedics found him.

His landlady and I stood watching the ambulance taillights disappear. "God bless poor old Davey," she said.

Look, I don't know what happens when people die. I'd like to think we go to a big party up yonder. A place with rodeos, big symphonies, kids born into normal families. But I guess the real reason I'm writing this is because sometimes I think about people I've known. People like you.

I don't know what you're facing today—everyone faces something. I don't know how much longer you'll have strength to keep kicking against it. In fact, I don't know anything. But no matter who you are, who you've lost, or what your religious persuasion, I want you to know something.

This isn't all there is.

God bless you.

SNEADS, FLORIDA

It was a classified ad in one of those nickel newspapers. It read:

"Gray Ford. Half-ton. Stick-shift. Some rust. Needs TLC. Sneads, Florida. $800."

My pal called about it. He needed a truck in a bad way. His old one had gone to be with Jesus, his wife was pregnant, and he'd just lost his job.

And in the days before texting, the only way to do business was to use the interstate.

Before we left, he went to the bank. He liquidated his account into a wallet-full of eight hundred dollars.

I gave him a ride. We stopped at a gas station outside Cottondale. He filled my tank, then paid inside. He bought two sticks of beef jerky, two scratch-off lottos.

Thoughtful.

After a two-hour ride we hit a dirt road leading to a farmhouse that sat on several acres of green. Out front: an old man, smoking. He was bony, friendly-faced, tall.

The truck was ugly, painted gray to hide rust. The bumpers were missing, the interior smelled like oyster stew.

"Runs good," the man said.

"I'll take it," my buddy answered.

He reached for his wallet. And that's when it happened.

His pocket was empty.

My friend went nuts. He retraced his steps. We tore apart my truck, dug through seats, and cussed. When he finally gave up, he sat cross-legged on the ground. He cried until his face looked raw.

The elderly man sat beside him. He wrapped his arms around him. It had been a long time since a man had done that sort of thing to my pal. He was a fatherless orphan, like me.

When things calmed down, the man's eyes were red and puffy. He wiped his face and said, "C'mon, son, nothin's THAT bad."

My pal didn't answer.

The elderly man removed keys from his pocket and placed them in my friend's hand.

He said, "Listen, that thing's gonna need an oil change when you get home."

And then he hugged him hard enough to break him.

Anyway, that was a long time ago. I haven't seen my buddy in a hundred years—I'll bet his baby is already drawing Social Security by now.

Still, I've replayed his story in my mind until I've worn out the record. Because the truth is, the world isn't all flowers and rainbows. It's angry, mean-spirited, selfish. Another day; another good man dies. I'm no fool. I watch the news.

I know people have quit hoping. I know it's fashionable to believe this place has already landed in the outhouse. I know a lot of folks think love is an elaborate myth that comes straight from a Sunday-school lesson.

Well.

They're dead wrong.

And I'll bet eight hundred bucks on it.

REAL GIRLS

I just saw a television commercial that made me blush. The starved-looking swimsuit model on the screen wasn't wearing enough to floss her teeth with. I don't even know what the ad was selling—nor do I give a flannel.

Look, I'm not complaining. God help me, I'm not.

Yes I am.

What happened to women? I'm talking real figures and Grecian curvature? Once upon a time, girls had meat on their bones and weren't afraid to finish off a fried chicken drumstick? There wasn't a thing wrong with them.

My grandaddy once said, "Boy, the best advice I can give you: marry a woman who wears cotton panties and eats until she's good and full."

I gave a confused look.

He went on, "The sort of lady who wears expensive, satin britches and eats like a bird, she's trouble."

Trouble.

I've thought about that my whole life. Subsequently, I also learned Grandaddy's advice isn't something you bring up at your mama's Bible study—unless you want the Jesus slapped out of you with a hairbrush.

Admittedly, I'm inclined to agree with Grandaddy. But then, I come from a long line of redneck women. Strong and firm ladies, who could clean a chicken carcass, sweep the porch, hang laundry, and kiss your skinned knees during the same afternoon.

We've done modern girls wrong.

My friend's teenage daughter claims she's afraid to eat in front of boys. She's a brunette beauty whose PE teacher told her she was overweight. The entire class calculated body-fat percentages on computers.

This played havoc on the girl's mind. She quit eating suppers, started living at the gym. She even began vomiting after meals. One day, she passed out at school. They sent her to a shrink.

The doc suggested putting her on a diet.

God help us. I'm no psychologist, but we don't need any more carb-counting. We need women unafraid. We need less size-zeroes, less two-pieces, and more women proud of their iron skillets. Fewer X-rated commercials, more Aunt Bee reruns.

A woman is a human being. She has a real face—one that looks good without makeup. She has a figure that's unique. And an appetite. For life, love, humor, and hickory smoked ham.

She's designed to laugh until she snorts, to enjoy rich desserts, and to cuss from time to time. She wears what she likes, talks as loud as she wants, sips beer from a can, and sees the universe in her own way.

She's a female. God created her for changing the world, raising families, and making a boy feel like a man.

She's not perfect. She's downright flawless.

To hell with swimsuit ads.

SAINTS YOU FIND IN WINN DIXIE

I saw her in the Winn-Dixie parking lot. I was walking in. She was coming out. I recognized her right off.

I've changed a lot over the years. She hasn't. She looks like she did when I sat in her English class long ago. White hair, pearls, dressed to the nines.

She taught night classes.

Back then, I'd arrive on campus early. I'd eat supper in my truck—a pimento cheese sandwich—while doing homework. Then, I'd change my work-shirt and go inside.

Hers was the only class I didn't hate.

She wasn't an overly friendly woman. And because of this, several students didn't care for her. But she was kind to me during a time when I felt lost.

And in my book that's a good teacher.

Though as it happens, I'm not exactly what you'd call a good pupil. I never have been. In my school career, I've spent most of my accredited hours trying to figure out whether the professors were speaking graduate-level Pig-Latin.

After my first semester with her, I signed up for her English II course. After I graduated, I took two more of her classes, just because I liked her.

My mama asked why on earth I'd go to the trouble,

taking classes I didn't need.

I hate goodbyes, I guess.

I remember when her husband passed. She didn't come to school for a week. The entire night-class-full of construction grunts and cocktail waitresses buried her desk in sympathy cards.

I went to the funeral with another student. We both wore neckties. She cried when she saw us.

We returned the favor.

The night of our last class, I remember her saying, "I've enjoyed having you, you're a smart boy."

Smart.

That might seem like a small word. But she's one of the only teachers who's ever gone and said that. That single kindhearted sentence has done me a lot of good over the years.

That evening, she asked what I'd be doing with my degree.

I told her I hadn't attended college for a career, but because of a promise I'd made to a dead man.

Today she was that same woman.

She patted my cheek and said, "You look so old."

I blushed. We embraced.

I offered to roll her shopping buggy to her vehicle. I loaded her groceries. We talked. She still teaches night-classes, I still drive an ugly truck.

Before we said goodbye, she said, "You know, when I first became a teacher I thought I was gonna make a big difference in the world, but somewhere along the way, I realized that's not who I am."

I gave her one final hug and told her I disagreed.

Because she sure as hell made a difference in my life.

DOTHAN, ALABAMA

I'm in Dothan, Alabama, eating at Annie Pearl's Home Cooking Restaurant. They tell me this is the only spot in town where you can get a decent liver covered in respectable gravy.

They were right.

I'm in a good mood. Not just because of the liver. But because earlier today, an eighty-six-year-old woman with Parkinson's hugged my neck. She said in a weak voice, "Your daddy sure is proud of you, young man."

It unsettled me.

Daddy's been dead for two thirds of my life. Nobody's ever told me that.

Let alone a stranger.

So we went out for smother-fried liver. I've already eaten fifty pounds of the stuff. Also: butter beans, turnip greens, and enough biscuits to qualify as a misdemeanor.

This restaurant is empty, except for a few camouflage hats and their wives.

Our waitress is Kendall. She's a breath of fresh air. She visits every table, speaking to customers as friendly as you'd talk to your cousins.

I overhear her say things like: "How's your sister doin' after her divorce?" Or: "Lordy, girl, did you see So-And-So's engagement ring?"

Or: "Congratulations, Dalene, I heard your nephew made bail last week."

People say sweet things in this town.

It's not a small place—this is the New York City of lower Alabama. But it's rural.

There's a Feed and Seed next to the Piggly Wiggly, muddy trucks in the movie-theater parking lot. At gas stations: old men in ten-gallon hats who can't figure out pump card-readers.

I spoke at the Houston County Library today. It was a small crowd. I met good people. Men like Fletcher Moore—an old man who talks so loud it makes you grin.

I got introduced to white-haired women who grew up barefoot, who still remember handpumps on kitchen sinks. I met ladies with antique names like Delphinia, Eugenia, Thomisina, Betty Sue, and Viola Ann.

I shook hands with a man in a neon orange cap who gave me a frozen Ziplock bag of venison. I met a handful of teachers, a few Auburn fans, one horse farrier.

And an eighty-six-year-old woman.

The little lady hugged me so hard I felt her tremble. She delivered a whispered message. Then, she planted a shaky kiss on me.

I won't lie, I've lived most of my life wishing things had turned out another way. I've spent too much time wondering if the dead fella whose name I share would be proud of me.

Not today.

Today, I ate liver for supper and smiled. Today, my waitress refilled my sweet tea and called me, "baby." Today, an eighty-six-year-old Alabamian, who shakes like an oak leaf, gave some kid a message from the Other Side.

I never even caught her name.

But I'm sure as hell glad I came to Dothan, or I might've missed it.

THE TALKER

Lunchtime—a service station somewhere in Alabama. He was chatty. Too chatty. He was as tall as a boom-truck, big ears, dirt smudges all over his work clothes, a wide smile, and some gray on his temples.

The place was crowded. His voice was the loudest one in the room. He talked to anyone who'd listen. And it drew looks from other folks in line.

If he'd been this talkative in a Northern city—say, the wrong side of New York—someone might've tried to quiet him by landing one on his chin. Though chin-level is five feet above eye-level.

Maybe six.

As it happens, New York is where he just left. Last month. But he's not from there, he's from here. And to listen to his accent sounds like an afternoon holding a fruit jar.

He was a marine. Semper Fi. He's retired now. When he left, the first thing he did was travel here. He couldn't get back home fast enough to see his mother.

"You know what I miss most?" he said, between bites of his gas-station hotdog. "Not being in a hurry. You take it for granted. In a city, they's in a hurry for every-damn-thing."

Every damn thing.

Yeah. I know what he means. I know some folks in such hurries they can't use microwaves without cussing at them.

My new buddy went on to explain that he'd spent a lot of time traveling between New York and overseas. While across the world last year, his mother passed. It happened suddenly, and it about killed him.

"I had a service for her, where I's stationed. Our chaplain said a few words over a picture I printed on the computer. All the guys in my unit came. I was supposed to be tough, but I cried pretty hard."

His eyes got glassy when he said it.

He visited her grave within the first five minutes of crossing the county line. He suffocated her in flowers. He wept. Then he stayed for half the day—until he got dizzy from hunger.

"You know," he went on. "I 'member when I left for basic training. Mama was so proud'a me, she told me, 'William, do good work, and be somebody.' I promised her I would. She made me the person I am today."

By the time he paid the cashier, he'd already finished his hotdog and was halfway into his Mountain Dew. He turned around to bid me goodbye, winked, and said, "Have a good day, boss. And God bless you."

Well, boss.

God just did.

HUMBLE PEOPLE

I believe humble people will take over the world. Maybe that seems like a strange thing to say. Just hear me out.

Eventually, I think modest people will own every football stadium, steel factory, brewery, peanut farm, fishing hole, longleaf forest, Tennessee mountain, elementary school, and low-level supervisor job at Walmart.

It will take some time. Maybe hundreds of years. But these folks are cropping up everywhere. They're biding their time.

I'm talking about people like my cousin. At family gatherings, he doesn't even fix a plate for himself. He fills yours instead, and when you're finished, he'll take it to the sink.

At the end of the night, you'll find him and his wife doing dishes.

People like Danny. Who started a company with his friend. After fifteen years, his friend elected himself president and started buying new cars every few weeks.

They gave Danny a pay cut.

Danny told me, "When they fired me, it was kind of a blessing. I'm just not smart enough to run a big business."

He's blessed to be a janitor now.

People like Lisa. Who has spent most of her life

living in a two-bedroom trailer. She has five kids. Five. No husband. She jokingly calls herself a failure.

Well, joke all you want, Lisa. But your daughter is no failure. She graduated from the University of Alabama on a full scholarship. Your oldest son did the same thing. Your youngest boy is a missionary in Chile.

Some failure.

Then there's Billy, who stutters. His father beat him for it. Also, Amanda, who towers over her eighth-grade class, who thinks she's fat, who speaks in a whisper.

Caroline, who's wanted to be an artist her whole life, but is too busy caring for her disabled husband to have time.

Melissa, too unselfish to take the last biscuit at breakfast this morning. Ricky, a richly talented human being, and too good-hearted to believe it. Lyle, who refuses to be called Doctor. Paulo Sanchez, the man who mows lawns for a living.

Not just these, but anyone who sits at the kid's table instead of the head. Who tips waitresses too much. Who throws dozens of birthday parties for friends, but has never had one of their own.

Folks with calloused hands. Who have raised children to think more for others than for themselves. Single parents. Underprivileged. Handicapped. The deaf, mute, blind, grieving, sad, awkward, embarrassed, depressed. And anyone who's ever been abused.

The world might ignore you now, but it can't forever. Your self-doubt is your strength. This place will be yours one day.

Just hold on.

Your turn is next.

SMALL-TOWN BELLES

Crestview, Florida—Cracker Barrel is slow for lunch. There aren't enough folks here to form a baseball team.

I'm sitting alone at a two-top. The elderly woman at the table beside me is also by herself. We're both looking at the phony gas fireplace. It's not all that cold outside.

But a phony fire is better than no fire at all.

We get to talking. I can't tell how old she is, exactly, and it would be rude to ask. She's a small-town Belle. Women like her would rather be shot and quartered than discuss age with anyone who is not a board-certified physician.

What I do know about her:

She's wearing the same kind of perfume everyone's granny does. I don't know what this stuff is called, but the smell makes me smile.

Also, she's dressed to the nines. Pearls. Her handbag matches her blouse.

We make friends.

She orders a breakfast for lunch. She tells me she's been fasting because she had blood work done this morning.

It doesn't take long to learn she's a widow. But her husband died long ago while her kids were young.

"I didn't have time to remarry," she says. "I was too busy figuring out what was for dinner."

Then, she talks about her kids. And you ought to see this woman's face beam.

One of her sons is an attorney. The other is a restaurant manager. Her daughter is a sales-rep. All three have moved. Two went to Birmingham, I forget where her daughter moved to.

When she talks, I notice something in her voice. It's impossible to miss. She's lonely.

"I loved being a mother," she explains. "It's so hard, especially when you're single. But you live for your kids. You do it for so long, you don't even think of yourself as a woman anymore, you're just *Mama*."

This mama did whatever she could to get by. She was a working woman. And even though she never sought higher education, she paid for two university tuitions—the degrees half-belong to her.

She eats slow. I'm already finished before she's even touched her hash-brown casserole. But I'm not leaving just yet because I don't have anywhere to be.

And it's been a while since she's had an audience.

She removes a smartphone from her purse. She squints at the screen and hands it to me. "These're my daughter's kids."

"Beautiful," I say.

"They're coming to visit me next weekend. I've been working to get my house ready."

And even though she doesn't say it, she doesn't have to. She wishes they lived closer.

This is a woman whose children are her universe. She guided them through the hell of childhood. She's a hero. One who cooked, washed, mopped, gave baths, spanked, and kissed skinned elbows. She was born to love.

Now she eats alone.

I ask how long her daughter's going to be in town.

She smiles big. "As long as it takes her to find a job. She's moving in with me next month."

Well.

I thank her for the conversation. I feel like I ought to hug her, but I don't. Instead, I thank the Almighty for kids who come back home. And for mamas.

I leave a tip.

Lunch is on me, ma'am.

ABOUT THE AUTHOR

Sean Dietrich is a columnist and novelist, known for his commentary on life in the American South. His work has appeared in Southern Living, The Tallahassee Democrat, Good Grit, South Magazine, Yellowhammer News, the Bitter Southerner, Thom Magazine, The Mobile Press Register, and he has authored nine books

Made in the USA
Las Vegas, NV
21 April 2024